B

AIRSHIPS AND FLYING MACHINES

BY

GERTRUDE BACON

1905

British Library Cataloguing-in-Publication Data
A catalogue record for this book is available from the
British Library

The Early History of Flight

In the 21st century—the age of the budget airline—where quick and reliable air travel is available to a large segment of society, it seems hard to comprehend that it is less than 250 years since the first human took to the skies. Throughout history, our species has viewed the birds with wonder, envy, and an irresistible urge for the freedom they posses. Many tried to attain that freedom, and many failed. From the legends of Icarus to the sketches of Leonardo da Vinci, great minds have occupied themselves with replicating the feathered wing—their designs running parallel to the images of heavenly angels in the arts. The principle of creating lift with a wing was of course sound, but it had to wait for the science of the twentieth century to become practical. Until then, a different line of enquiry had to be followed. This spawned the "lighter-than-air period" of aviation.

The concept of heated air being used to generate lift goes back as far as third century C.E. China when Kongming lanterns were used to send messages. It was only in the eighteenth century however, with the innovations of a couple of French paper-makers, the Montgolfier brothers, that the principle was utilised as a means of transport. It was in their balloon, on 21st November 1783, that Pilâtre de Rozier and the Marquis d'Arlandes became the first humans to join the birds and traverse the skies. This ascent was soon followed by that of Charles and Robert in the first hydrogen balloon. The seed had been sown and many others took up the gauntlet to set new records, make scientific observations, and entertain the masses.

In this early-industrial age, the excitement for new technology was immense, and thousands of people would gather and pay to watch these "aeronauts" ascend. The public appetite for all things balloon related led to the coining of the term "Balloonomania", and the enthusiasm for seeing these aviators lift off in their majestic craft is comparable to that of the dawn of the space age in the mid-twentieth century.

As with all forays into the unknown, ballooning took its toll. Several pioneers lost their lives and many more came close. Over the years however, science, and the designs of the balloons became better understood, and although the frontiers of ballooning remain a risky endeavour, many people all over the world now enjoy ballooning as a pastime.

At the beginning of the 20th century, a new technology took to the air that would revolutionise aeronautics. When the 'Wright Flyer', designed by Orville and Wilbur Wright, made its maiden flight in 1903, travelling a distance of 120 feet, it set the tone for the future of aviation. Aeroplanes soon became the prominent force in air travel, developing both commercial and military applications very early on in their existence.

A world without flight now seems hard to imagine and I hope the reader is intrigued to find out more about the exciting and fascinating subject of aviation history.

THE AUTHORESS, HER FATHER, AND MR. SPENCER
MAKING AN ASCENT.

Frontispiece.

CONTENTS

BALLOONS, AIRSHIPS, AND FLYING MACHINES

CHAPTER I

THE ORIGIN OF BALLOONING

ONE November night in the year 1782, so the story runs, two brothers sat over their winter fire in the little French town of Annonay, watching the grey smoke-wreaths from the hearth curl up the wide chimney. Their names were Stephen and Joseph Montgolfier, they were papermakers by trade, and were noted as possessing thoughtful minds and a deep interest in all scientific knowledge and new discovery. Before that night — a memorable night, as it was to prove—hundreds of millions of people had watched the rising smoke-wreaths of their fires without drawing any special inspiration from the fact; but on this particular occasion, as Stephen, the younger of the brothers, sat and gazed at the familiar sight, the question flashed across his mind, " What is the hidden power that makes those curling smoke-wreaths rise upwards, and could I not employ it to make other things rise also ? "

Then and there the brothers resolved on an

MEDALLION SHOWING BROTHERS MONTGOLFIER.

experiment. They made themselves a small fire of some light fuel in a little tin tray or chafing-dish, and over the smoke of it they held a large paper-bag. And to their delight they saw the bag fill out and make a feeble attempt to rise. They were surely on the eve of some great invention; and yet, try as they would, their experiment would not quite succeed, because the smoke in the bag always became too cool before there was enough in it to raise it from the table. But presently, while they were thus engaged, a neighbour of theirs, a widow lady, alarmed by seeing smoke issuing from their window, entered the room, and after watching their fruitless efforts for some while, suggested that they should fasten the tray on to the bottom of the bag. This was done, with the happy result that the bag immediately rose up to the ceiling; and in this humble fashion the first of all balloons sailed aloft.

That night of 1782, therefore, marks the first great step ever made towards the conquest of the sky. But to better understand the history of "Aeronautics"—a word that means "the sailing of the air"—we must go back far beyond the days of the Montgolfier brothers. For in all times and in all ages men have wanted to fly. David wished for the wings of a dove to fly away and be at rest, and since his time, and before it, how many have not longed to take flight and sail away in the boundless, glorious realms above, to explore the fleecy clouds, and to float free in the blue vault of heaven.

And since birds achieve this feat by means of wings, man's first idea was to provide himself with wings also.   But here he was at once doomed to disappointment.   It is very certain that by his own natural strength alone a man will never propel himself through the air with wings like a bird, because he is made quite differently.   A bird's body is very light compared with its size.   The largest birds in existence weigh under thirty pounds.   A man's body, on the contrary, is very heavy and solid.   The muscles that work a bird's wing are wonderfully powerful and strong, far stronger in proportion than the muscles of a man's arm.   To sustain his great weight in the air, a man of eleven stone would require a pair of wings nearly twenty feet in span. But the possession of such mighty wings alone is not enough.   He must also possess bodily strength to keep them in sufficient motion to prevent him from falling, and for this he would require at least the strength of a horse.

Such strength a man has never possessed, or can ever hope to; but even as it is, by long practice and great effort, men have succeeded at different times, not exactly in flying, but in helping themselves along considerably by means of wings.   A man is said to have flown in this way in Rome in the days of Nero.   A monk in the Middle Ages, named Elmerus, it is stated, flew about a furlong from the top of a tower in Spain, another from St. Mark's steeple in Venice, and another from Nuremburg. But the most successful attempt ever made in this direction was accomplished about 200 years ago by a French locksmith of the name of Besnier. He had made for himself a pair of light wooden oars, shaped like the double paddle of a canoe, with cup-like blades at either end. These he placed over his shoulders, and attached also to his feet, and

BESNIER AND HIS OARS.

then casting himself off from some high place, and violently working his arms and legs so as to buffet the air downwards with his paddles, he was able to raise himself by short stages from one height to another, or skim lightly over a field or river. It is said that subsequently Besnier sold his oars to a mountebank, who performed most successfully with them at fairs and festivals.

But it was soon clear that the art of human

flight was not to be achieved by such means; and when men found that they were unable to soar upwards by their own bodily strength alone, they set about devising some apparatus or machine which should carry them aloft. Many ancient philosophers bent their minds to the inventing of a machine for this purpose. One suggested that strong flying birds, such as eagles or vultures, might be harnessed to a car, and trained to carry it into the sky. Another gravely proposed the employment of " a little imp "—for in those days the existence of imps and demons was most firmly believed in.   A third even went so far as to give an actual *recipe* for flying, declaring that " if the eggs of the larger description of swans, or leather balls stitched with fine thongs, be filled with nitre, the purest sulphur, quicksilver, or kindred materials which rarefy by their caloric energy, and if they externally resemble pigeons, they will easily be mistaken for flying animals." (!)

The first man who appeared to have any inkling of the real way of solving the problem of a " flying chariot," and who in dim fashion seems to have foreshadowed the invention of the balloon, was that wonderful genius, Roger Bacon, the Learned Friar of Ilchester, the inventor or re-inventor of gunpowder, who lived in the thirteenth century. He had an idea — an idea which was far ahead of his times, and only proved to be true hundreds of years after — that the earth's atmosphere was an actual substance or "true fluid," and as such he supposed it to have an upper surface as the sea has, and on this upper surface he thought an airship might float, even as a boat floats on the top of the water. And to make his airship rise upwards to reach this upper sea, he said one must employ "a large hollow globe of copper or other similar metal wrought extremely thin, to have it as light as possible, and filled with *ethereal air* or liquid fire."

It is doubtful whether Bacon had very clear ideas of what he meant by "ethereal air." But, whether by accident or insight, he had in these words hit upon the true principle of the balloon—a principle only put into practice five centuries later. He saw that a body would rise upwards through the air if it were filled with something lighter than air, even as a body will rise upwards through the water if it is made of, or filled with, something lighter than water. We know that if we throw an empty bottle tightly corked into the sea it does not sink, but rises upwards, because it is filled with air, which is lighter than water. In the same way exactly a light bag or balloon which is filled with some gas which is lighter than air will not stay on the surface of the ground, but will rise upwards into the sky to a height which depends upon its weight and buoyancy.

Later philosophers than Bacon came to the same conclusion, though they do not seem to have seen matters more clearly. As recently as 1755 a certain learned French priest actually suggested that since the air on the top of high mountains is known to be lighter than that at an ordinary level, men might ascend to these great heights and bring down the light air "in constructions of canvas or cotton." By means of this air he then proposed to fly a great machine, which he describes, and which seems to have been as large and cumbersome as Noah's Ark. Needless to say, the worthy Father's proposal has never yet been put into practice.

But it is time now that we return to the two brothers Montgolfier and their paper-bag of smoke. Their experiments proved at once that in smoke they had found something which was lighter than air, and which would, therefore, carry a light weight upwards. But of what this something was they had, at the time, but a confused idea. They imagined that the burning fuel they had used had given off some special light gas, with the exact nature of which they were unacquainted. The very word gas, be it here said, was in those days almost unknown, and of different gases, their nature and properties, most people had but the very vaguest notions.

And so for some time the Montgolfiers and their followers supposed that the presence of this mysterious gas was necessary to the success of their experiments, and they were very careful about always using special kinds of fuel, which they supposed gave off this gas, to inflate their bags. Later experiments proved, however, what every one now knows, that the paper - bag rose, not because of the gases given off by the fire, but by reason of the hot air with which it became filled. Nearly all substances, no matter how solid, expand more or less under the influence of heat, and air expands very greatly indeed. By thus expanding heated air becomes lighter than the surrounding air, and, because it is lighter, rises upwards in the atmosphere, and continues to rise until it has once more regained the average temperature.

Encouraged by the success of their first humble experiment, the Montgolfiers next tried their paper-bag in the open air, when to their delight it sailed upwards to a height of 70 feet. The next step was to make a much larger craft of 600 cubic feet capacity and spherical in shape, which they called a "Balloon," because it was in appearance like a large, round, short-necked vessel used in chemistry which was technically known by that name. This great bag, after being inflated, became so powerful that it broke loose from its moorings, and floated proudly upwards 600 feet and more, and came down in an adjoining field. After a few more suc-

MONTGOLFIER'S BALLOON.

cessful trials the brothers thought that the time had come to make known their new invention. Accordingly they constructed a great balloon of 35 feet in diameter, and issued invitations to the public to come and see the inflation. This was successfully made over a fire of chopped straw and wool, and the giant rose up into the sky amid the deafening applause of a huge multitude, and after attaining a height of 7000 feet, fell to the ground a mile and a half away.

The news of this marvellous event spread like wild-fire throughout the kingdom, and soon not only all France, but all Europe also, was ringing with the tidings. The French Royal Academy of Sciences immediately invited Stephen Montgolfier to Paris, and provided him with money to repeat his experiment. He accordingly constructed a yet larger machine, which stood no less than 72 feet high, had it most magnificently painted and decorated and hung with flags, and sent it up at Versailles in the presence of the King and all his court.

This particular balloon is noteworthy as having been the first of all balloons to carry living passengers into the air. They were three in number, a sheep, a cock, and a duck. Breathlessly the assembled multitude watched these innocent victims placed in the basket and soar calmly and majestically above their heads; and eagerly they followed the balloon to where it fell half a mile away to learn their fate. Would they have been suffocated in those upper regions of the air which no human being had yet explored, or would they be dashed to pieces in the descent? But they found the trio quite uninjured ; the unimaginative sheep grazing quietly, and the duck cheerfully quacking. Forthwith the cry then arose that it was time for a man to hazard the ascent, and King Louis, who, like every one else, was vastly excited over the wonder, suggested that two criminals then lying under sentence of death should be sent aloft.

But now a brave French gentleman—M. Pilâtre de Rozier, a name ever to be remembered in the history of the conquest of the air —uprose in indignation. " Shall vile criminals have the first glory of rising into the sky!" he cried, and then and there he proudly claimed for himself the honour of being first among mortals in the history of the world to sail the air. His courageous resolve was wildly applauded, and forthwith preparations were commenced for the new venture. A yet larger balloon was made, in height as tall as a church tower, with a mouth 15 feet across. Around the mouth was fastened a gallery of wicker-work, three feet wide, to hold the passengers, and below all was slung with chains an iron brazier of burning fuel.

By way of precaution, when all was com-

plete De Rozier made a few short captive
excursions, the balloon being fastened to
earth by a rope. But all proving satisfactory,
he decided to hazard a "right away" trip on
the 21st of November 1783, when he was also
to be accompanied by an equally courageous
fellow-countryman, the Marquis d'Arlandes.
It would be difficult to conceive a more daring
and perilous enterprise than these two brave
Frenchmen set themselves. They were to
venture, by an untried way, into unknown
realms where no mortal had been before;
they were to entrust their lives to a frail
craft whose capabilities had never yet been
tested, and at a giddy height they were to
soar aloft with an open fire, which at any
moment might set light to the inflammable
balloon and hurl them to destruction.

Wild indeed was the applause of the crowd
as the mighty craft, after due inflation, rose
majestically into the sky, carrying with it its
two brave voyagers—

the first that ever burst
Into that silent sea;

and with what anxiety was its course followed
as, rising rapidly to a height of 3000 feet, it
drifted away on an upper current which bore
it right over the city of Paris. The travellers
themselves experienced various excitements
during their adventurous trip. They had
constantly to stir the fire and feed it with

fresh fuel; they had also with wet sponges continually to extinguish the flames when the light fabric from time to time ignited. At one period they feared descending into the river or on the house-tops, at another a sharp shock gave them the impression that

AN EARLY HYDROGEN BALLOON.

their balloon had burst. But they came safely in the end through all perils and alarms, descending quietly, after a voyage of twenty-five minutes' duration, five miles from their starting-place.

Thus was invented and perfected in the course of less than a year the first of all craft which carried man into the sky—the Hot-Air or Montgolfier Balloon. To this day large hot-air balloons inflated by the same methods employed a hundred years ago occasionally take passengers aloft. Indeed, there now seems a likelihood that the use of the Montgolfier balloon will be largely revived for military purposes, since, with modern improvements, it would appear to be more quickly and easily inflated than a gas balloon in time of warfare. With miniature hot-air balloons we are all familiar, for every schoolboy has made them for himself of coloured papers, and watched them float away on the breeze with as much admiration and delight as the two brothers of Annonay watched their bag first float upwards to the ceiling.

But almost before the invention of the hot-air balloon had been completed, and before Pilâtre de Rozier had made his ascent, a rival craft had appeared upon the scene, to which we must more specially refer in the next chapter.

CHAPTER II

THE COMING OF THE GAS BALLOON

DURING the time of which we are speaking there was living in London a famous chemist named Henry Cavendish. He was the son of

a nobleman, and a very rich man; but he
shut himself up entirely from the world, and
devoted his whole time and energies to the
study of science. So afraid was he of being
interrupted in his work that he lived the life
of a hermit, commanding his servants to keep
out of his sight on pain of dismissal, and
ordering his dinner daily by means of a
note placed on the hall table. In the year
1760—twenty-two years before the Montgolfier brothers began their experiments—this
eccentric man had discovered what was then
known as "inflammable air," but what we
now call hydrogen gas.

Cavendish's experiments proved that hydrogen is the lightest of all known substances,
being about fourteen times lighter than at-
mospheric air; and soon after he had made
known his researches, it occurred to a certain
Dr. Black of Edinburgh that if a sufficiently
thin and light bladder were filled with this
"inflammable air" it would rise upwards.
Dr. Black even went so far as to order a
special bladder to be prepared for the purpose; but by the time it was ready he was
busy with other work, and the experiment
was never made; otherwise it is extremely
probable that the honour of inventing the
balloon would have been won for this country,
and not for France.

A little later Tiberius Cavallo, an Italian
chemist living in England, came yet nearer

to the great invention, for he filled a number of soap-bubbles with the newly discovered gas, and saw them float high into the air. He did not, however, think at the time that his experiments would lead to any practical result, and so the matter dropped entirely, until the world was suddenly electrified by the tidings of the wonderful hot-air balloon invented by the brothers Montgolfier at Annonay.

The news of this discovery recalled to the minds of many the almost forgotten experiments of the past, and it was forthwith suggested that balloons might be inflated with hydrogen gas more successfully than with hot air. It was resolved immediately to put this theory to the test. A large subscription to defray expenses was raised in Paris without difficulty, for men's minds were keen on the new-found art of sailing the sky; and M. Charles, Professor of Experimental Philosophy, and two brothers, the Messrs. Roberts, well - known mechanicians, were appointed to construct a suitable balloon and inflate it by the new method.

But they were immediately confronted with a difficulty. Hydrogen being the lightest and most subtle of gases, they were at a loss to know of what material to make their balloon, to prevent the gas escaping. After several failures they eventually constructed a bag of a special kind of silk, and coated it all over with a varnish made of indiarubber dissolved in turpentine. As they found great difficulty in manufacturing large quantities of hydrogen, they were forced to make their bag a comparatively small one, about thirteen feet in diameter. On the 25th of August 1783

ATTACK ON THE FIRST CHARLIER BALLOON.

the bag was successfully filled, and the ascent was made in Paris in the presence of an enormous crowd. The little balloon rose upwards with immense rapidity, until it was lost to sight in the clouds. Ascending yet higher, it presently burst, and came to the earth in a village, fifteen miles away, after a voyage of three-quarters of an hour.

In the field where the balloon fell a party of peasants were at work; at its approach they fled in abject terror. From a safe distance they watched the strange new monster settle to earth and lie prone, and then they cautiously drew nearer to inspect it. The silk still heaved with the escaping gas, and the countrymen were fully convinced that an actual living creature of mysterious nature lay before them. One man seized his gun and fired full at it, and then supposing it to be mortally wounded, they all rushed in with flails and pitchforks to complete its destruction, finally tying it to the tail of a horse, who galloped with it all over the country, tearing it to shreds. It was small wonder that after such an occurrence the French Government issued a proclamation to the people, telling them that these aeronautical experiments were to be repeated, and warning them not to be alarmed if they saw a balloon in the air, since it was a perfectly harmless machine filled with gas, and incapable of injuring any one.

This event took place about three months after the first public ascent of the hot-air balloon. The new craft was immediately called a "Charlier," after its inventor, and to distinguish it from the "Montgolfier." There followed various exhibitions of the rival airships, and after the voyage of Pilâtre de Rozier and the Marquis D'Arlandes,

Messrs. Charles and Roberts resolved also to hazard an ascent in a balloon inflated with hydrogen.

A new machine was therefore constructed, which differed in many important details from all others which had previously been made. It was twenty-seven feet in diameter, of varnished silk, and over it was spread a net of cordage. Instead of a gallery to carry the passengers, as in the "Montgolfier," a car shaped like a boat was suspended from the net with ropes and hung a few feet below the balloon. A valve to let out the gas was also provided, and the voyagers carried in their car ballast and a barometer to indicate their height. It will thus be seen that this new balloon was in all practical details the same as the balloon of the present day.

The ascent took place on the 17th of December in Paris. Stephen Montgolfier was present, and launched a small hot-air balloon, which amused the onlookers and indicated the direction of the wind. Then MM. Charles and Roberts stepped into the car, and the balloon being liberated, they were immediately carried up to a height of 6000 feet, where a glorious panorama of Paris and the adjacent country was spread out before their delighted vision. After staying aloft about a couple of hours they descended to earth again, and Roberts got out of the car. Charles decided to continue the voyage awhile by himself, and, lightened of his companion's weight, the balloon this time rose to 10,500 feet. The sun had by this time set upon the earth, but at this height Charles saw it rise once more and set a second time. The thermometer fell far below freezing-point, and he was benumbed with cold and felt violent pains in his ears. When at his greatest elevation he was obliged to pull the valve to prevent the balloon from bursting, and eventually descended without mischance about seven miles from where Roberts had left him.

It would be well now to describe a little more fully the way in which the "Montgolfier" and "Charlier" balloons were inflated. Each of the rival methods had its advantages and also its disadvantages. In the case of the hot-air balloon a shallow pit was dug, in which a quick-burning fire of chopped wool and straw was lighted, and the bag simply suspended over it. The inflation was thus rapid, and its cost comparatively small; the great drawback being that as the bag was of very light material, it ran considerable risk of being ignited by the fire; and all the while it was filling it was the uncomfortable duty of an unfortunate attendant to stand actually inside, roasted with the heat and choked with the smoke, armed with a paddle with which to beat out the flames whenever the bag caught alight.

This danger of fire was done away with in the method of filling with hydrogen gas. The balloon, suspended from aloft as before, was connected by hose-pipes with a number of casks containing iron or zinc filings upon which dilute sulphuric acid was poured. The

FILLING A HOT AIR BALLOON.

effect of mixing these substances together is to set up a brisk chemical action, in the course of which hydrogen gas is given off. In this case the hydrogen thus liberated came through the pipes and filled the balloon. The great disadvantages of this method of filling—which, it may here be mentioned, is occasionally employed at the present day—are the long time it occupies, the great labour entailed, and the enormous expense.

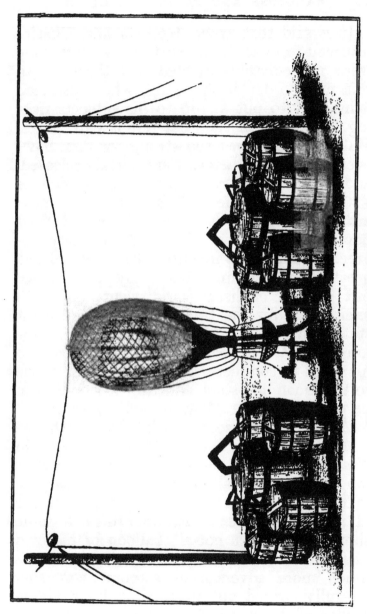

FILLING A HYDROGEN GAS BALLOON.

It is said that when Roberts and Charles returned from their adventurous voyage they were immediately arrested and thrown into prison by order of the King, who considered it his duty to put a stop to his subjects risking their lives in such dangerous enterprises. Public opinion was too strong for him, however, and the two heroes were quickly released, and Charles was rewarded by a pension of £200 a year for life.   This newly discovered art of sailing the heavens had indeed fired popular imagination to an extraordinary degree.   Probably no invention has ever aroused greater enthusiasm.   Not only all France but all the civilised world went wild with excitement for the time.   Most extravagant statements were made and written.   A new kingdom, it was declared, had been given to mankind to conquer; voyages might be made to the moon and stars, and now it would even be possible to take Heaven itself by storm!

Ascent after ascent took place with the "Montgolfier" and the "Charlier," both in France and in other countries; nor was it long before the balloon made its appearance in England.   In August of the next summer (1784) a Mr Tytler of Edinburgh made some short voyages in a hot-air balloon of his own manufacture, and in the following month a much more adventurous attempt was successfully carried out in London by a young Italian of the name of Vincent Lunardi.

Lunardi was at this time secretary to the Neapolitan Ambassador. He was keenly interested in the subject of ballooning, and presently became fired with a desire to repeat in England those aerial experiments which were creating such a sensation on the Continent. He was only a poor man, and great difficulties stood in the way of accomplishing his object. He had to excite public interest in his venture, to collect subscriptions to defray the cost of his balloon, which was to be a " Charlier," and to find a suitable site in London for the inflation

VINCENT LUNARDI.

and ascent. He met with disappointments and disasters enough to discourage a less enthusiastic man, but at length, after many troubles, on the 15th of September his balloon was ready and in process of filling in the grounds of the Honourable Artillery Company, in the city, where 150,000 people had assembled to witness the new wonder.

C

Still Lunardi's trials were not at an end. The balloon was advertised to ascend at a certain hour; but the supply of gas was insufficient, so that when the time came it was only partially filled, and a long delay ensued. The vast crowd—more than half inclined to believe the whole thing an imposture—began to grow very impatient and unruly, and it was only the presence of the Prince of Wales, afterwards George the Fourth, which kept them in restraint for another hour while the filling continued.

Even then the balloon was not full; but Lunardi felt he could wait no longer. He left behind him the companion who was to have accompanied him, substituted a smaller and lighter car, jumped inside and severed the ropes. Instantly the balloon rose high over the delighted city, as the crowd, led by the Prince himself, rent the air with their cheers. Wild was the excitement in every quarter. At Westminster King George the Third was in conference with Mr. Pitt and his other chief Ministers of State, but when it was known that Lunardi was in the sky the King exclaimed, " Gentlemen, we may resume our deliberations at pleasure, but we may never see poor Lunardi again!" and with one accord they adjourned to watch his progress through telescopes. Tradesmen rushed out of their shops, business men from their offices, even judge and jury from their courts.

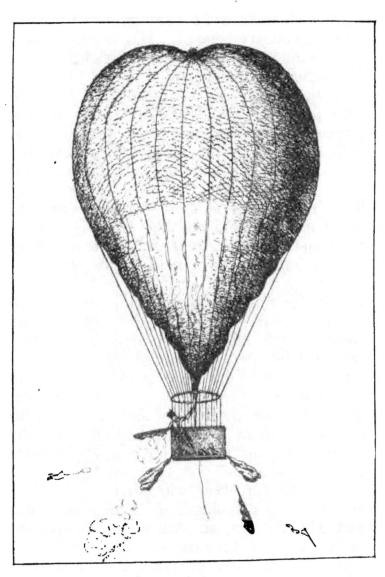

LUNARDI'S BALLOON.

Lunardi continued his voyage over the town into the country beyond. His balloon apparently attained a considerable height, for he found that the condensed moisture round the neck had frozen, and the gas, which to begin with had only two-thirds filled the balloon, presently expanded so much that he was obliged to untie the mouth to relieve the strain. He had taken up with him as companions a dog and a cat. The cat was very ill at ease in the cold of the upper regions, and he resolved to put her out; so, coming down to the ground, he handed her to a country woman standing in a field. Throwing out ballast, he then rose again and continued his voyage for some distance, eventually descending in a meadow near Ware. Some labourers were at work on the spot, but they at first refused to come near him, and a young woman was the first whom he could induce to help him out of his car. A stone with a long inscription, set up in a meadow in the parish of Standon, near Ware, marks to this day the place where the first of all English balloons touched ground.

The following year witnessed a yet bolder enterprise. Blanchard, a French aeronaut, and Dr. Jeffries, an American, determined on an attempt to cross the Channel. On a winter's day, early in 1785, they had their balloon inflated with hydrogen at Dover and boldly cast off to sea. The cold air appeared to chill the gas more than they had foreseen, and long before they were across the Channel their balloon began settling down upon the water. They threw out all their ballast, then a number of books they were carrying, then their anchor, extra ropes, and other gear. Still it seemed very doubtful whether they would reach the French coast, and as a last resort they began even to throw away their clothes to lighten the balloon. Fortunately at this moment the balloon shot up into the air again, and eventually brought them down in safety near the forest of Guiennes.

So far, although several hundred ascents had been made, and in spite of the many and great dangers of the new-found art and the inexperience of the early voyagers, no fatal accident had marred the delight of sailing the skies. Disasters, however, were soon to come. It is sad to relate that the earliest to fall a victim was the brave Pilâtre de Rozier himself, the first of all men to go aloft in a balloon. Fired with a desire to emulate Blanchard and Jeffries, he decided that he himself would cross the Channel, this time from France to England; and to avoid, as he imagined, the cooling of the gas, which had so nearly proved disastrous on the previous occasion, he hit on the extraordinary idea of combining the principles of both the " Montgolfier " and "Charlier " balloons, and suspending a fire balloon beneath another filled with hydrogen gas. It

seems a remarkable thing to us now that no
one in those days saw the awful danger of
such a combination. The inevitable happened.
When the balloon was high in the air the
furnace of the hot-air machine set fire to
the highly inflammable hydrogen, a fearful
explosion followed, and De Rozier and his
companion were dashed to pieces.

CHAPTER III

FAMOUS BALLOON VOYAGES OF THE PAST

UNFORTUNATELY the death of Pilâtre de
Rozier was but the first of a series of fatal
accidents which marred the early years of
the history of ballooning. Shortly afterwards
another French aeronaut, going up in too
shallow a car, fell overboard when at a great
height and was killed. A little later Count
Zambeccari, an Italian, ascended in a hot-air
balloon, which, on coming near the earth,
became entangled in a tree. The furnace it
carried set fire to the silk. To escape from
the flames, the Count leapt to the ground
and was killed on the spot. A few years
after, Madame Blanchard, wife of the man
who first crossed the English Channel, made
a night ascent from Paris with a number of
fireworks hung from the car. These, in some

way, ignited the balloon, which fell to the
ground, killing the unfortunate lady in its fall.

On the other hand, many miraculous escapes
are on record.   One of the earliest balloonists
spent the night alone aloft in the midst of a
terrific thunder-storm, with the lightning flash-
ing all around him, and yet descended in safety
when morning broke.   M. Garnerin, a famous
French aeronaut of this date, also was lost in
a storm.   His balloon became unmanageable,
and borne to earth was dashed against a
mountain side, the occupant losing conscious-
ness, until the balloon, which had ascended
again, brought him safely down once more
many miles away.

A marvellous escape took place in 1808,
when two Italians ascended in a gas balloon
from Padua and attained a great height,
estimated as approaching 30,000 feet.   Here
the balloon burst, and came precipitately to
the ground; and yet, despite the terrific fall,
the aeronauts escaped with their lives.   The
explanation of this seeming impossibility was,
no doubt, the tendency which a balloon,
emptied of its gas, possesses to form a natural
parachute.   During a rapid fall the lower
part of the silk will, if loose, collapse into
the upper portion to form a kind of open
umbrella, and thus very effectually break the
descent.   Many balloonists have owed their
safety in similar accidents to this fortunate
fact.

The bursting of balloons when at high
altitudes has already been referred to as
happening on several previous occasions.   It
is a danger which is always present when a
balloon is aloft, unless due precautions are
taken, and the neglect of these precautions
has probably led to more ballooning accidents
than any other cause.   The explanation is
simply the varying pressure exerted upon the
bag of gas by the weight of the atmosphere.
When an inflated balloon is resting upon the
ground, the vast ocean of air above it is
pressing upon it with a weight of approxi-
mately fifteen pounds to the square inch, and
it is this pressure which prevents the enclosed
gas from expanding beyond a certain limit.
The balloon then rises high into the air, where
the weight of atmosphere pressing upon it is
much diminished.   The higher it rises the
less the pressure becomes, and the gas it
holds soon expands so much that, unless a
vent is provided for it, the balloon will burst.
At the present day the neck of a balloon is
always left wide open when the balloon is in
the air, to allow of the escape of the gas
during the ascent.

A perilous adventure befell Mr. Sadler, an
English aeronaut, in 1812, whilst attempting
to cross the Irish Channel.   He started from
Dublin with a wind which he hoped would
carry him to Liverpool, but had gone only
a short distance when he discovered a rent,

which seemed to be increasing, in the silk of his balloon. Climbing the rigging with difficulty, he contrived to tie up the hole with his neckcloth. He was by this time over the sea, and having passed near the Isle of Man, found himself, as evening was approaching, close to the coast of North Wales. Here he endeavoured to seek a landing, but just at the critical moment the wind shifted, as it frequently does in this treacherous Channel, and he was quickly blown out to sea again. There he remained for another hour vainly endeavouring to make the land, and then, despairing of the attempt and seeing five ships beneath him, he came boldly down on the water, trusting they would come to his assistance.

But he came down too far away from them, and one and all continued their course and took no notice. He was obliged, therefore, to throw out ballast and to rise into the air once more. The sun was now set upon the level of the water, but as the brave aeronaut rose he beheld it once more above the horizon, and was cheered by its beams. Presently he saw beneath him three more vessels, which signalled their willingness to help him, and he immediately came down on the sea again as close to them as he could. But the wind, now rising fast, caught the half empty silk of the balloon as it touched the waves, and bore it along over the surface of the water at a terrific pace; and although the vessels came after in full pursuit, they were unable to overtake it.

Mr. Sadler then dropped his grappling-iron to act as a drag, and this not proving sufficient, took off his clothes and tied them to the iron as a further expedient. Still the vessels failed to overhaul him as he sped over the waves, and he was at length forced to let out a quantity of the gas still remaining, and so cripple the balloon. But this was a dangerous move, for the car now instantly sank; and the unfortunate man had to clutch the hoop and then the netting, to keep himself above water. Chilled and exhausted, and frequently plunged beneath the waves, he was soon at the point of death; for the nearest ship, though now close at hand, fearful of becoming entangled in the netting, still held off. Fainting as he was, Mr. Sadler yet managed to summon strength to call to the sailors to run their bowsprit through the balloon to stop its course, and this being done, he was hauled on board more dead than alive.

Five years passed, and no more attempts were made to cross the treacherous Irish Sea, until Mr. Sadler's own son, Mr. Windham Sadler, determined himself to make the attempt which had so nearly cost his father his life. Choosing the same starting-ground for his venture, he left Dublin on the longest day of 1817, and, fortune favouring him, reached the Welsh coast not far from Holyhead, after a voyage of 70 miles, lasting five hours. This was the last attempt to cross the Irish Channel, until November 1902, when the Rev. J. M. Bacon and Mr. Percival Spencer, starting from Douglas, in the Isle of Man, landed in a rocky glen 15 miles beyond Dumfries, after a journey of 80 miles, accomplished in three hours. Brave Mr. Windham Sadler unhappily lost his life in a terrible balloon accident in 1824.

But a more celebrated balloonist, perhaps the most famous of all, had by this time come to the fore—Charles Green, fitly called "The Father of English Aeronautics." It was he who first introduced a new method of balloon-filling, which quickly revolutionised the whole art and practice. This was nothing more or less than the employment of ordinary household or coal gas for inflation, in place of the costly and dangerous hydrogen.

While balloons were inflated only with pure hydrogen—for the uncertain and dangerous method of filling with hot air was soon almost entirely abandoned—no great strides could be made in the art of sailing the skies. The filling of a large balloon eighty years ago cost no less than £250, and few people could be found willing to provide so much money for such a purpose. Coal gas, however, was by then to be found in every town of any consequence; and it was Green's suggestion that though this gas might be greatly inferior to pure hydrogen in buoyancy or "lifting power," it yet contained a sufficient quantity of hydrogen in it for all ordinary aeronautical purposes.

The coronation of King George the Fourth was the occasion chosen by Green to put his new scheme to the test and fill a balloon with coal gas. The experiment was entirely successful, and henceforward balloon ascents became much commoner throughout the world, for Green's discovery reduced the cost of filling tenfold, and the trouble and anxiety a hundredfold. Green himself became one of the most famous men of his day, and lived to make a thousand ascents, some of them of the most daring and exciting description.

The most celebrated event in all his career, however, was the voyage of the Great Nassau Balloon, in November 1836. This voyage created a tremendous sensation at the time, and has always been considered one of the most adventurous enterprises in the whole history of aeronautics. How it came about was as follows :—

The managers of the Vauxhall Gardens, London, had made, with Mr. Green's assistance, a very large and fine balloon of crimson silk, which stood eighty feet high and held 90,000 cubic feet of gas, and which would carry, if needed, more than twenty persons. After it was made the proprietors proposed exhibiting it in Paris, and there was some

THE GREAT NASSAU BALLOON.

question of how this valuable and fragile
property had best be conveyed so far. Mr.
Hollond, a young gentleman of considerable
wealth, and a great lover of adventure, at
once came forward, and proposed to take the
balloon to the Continent by sky. His offer was
accepted, and to make the ascent more noteworthy, it was decided to start from London
and cross the sea by night, making as long a
voyage as possible, although it was already
winter time, and such a venture had never
before been made.

Preparations were at once commenced. The
passengers were limited to three—Mr. Green,
who was to manage the balloon, Mr. Hollond,
and his friend Mr. Monck Mason. A ton of
ballast was to be carried, provisions for a whole
fortnight were laid in, and, since none could
tell to within a thousand miles or more where
they might be drifted, passports to every kingdom in Europe were obtained.

They left London late one November day,
and, rising under a north-west wind, skirted
the north of Kent. Passing presently over
Canterbury, they wrote a courteous message
to the mayor, and dropped it in a parachute.
Some time later, when the short autumn twi-
light was beginning to wane, they saw beneath
them the gleam of white waves, and knew
they had reached the boundary of the hitherto
much-dreaded sea. Immediately afterwards
they entered a heavy sea fog, which hid all

THE VOYAGE ACROSS THE CHANNEL.

things from their sight, and darkness and dead
silence reigned around.

This lasted for fifty minutes, when they
emerged from the cloud and found the bright
lights of Calais beneath them. It was then
quite dark, and they sped on through the
night over unknown towns and villages whose
lights gleamed fainter and fewer as the time
went on. Then once again they entered the
fog-bank, and for long hours no sign or sound
of earth reached them more.

As the night wore on they suddenly had
a startling and alarming experience. Their
balloon, which had been flying near the earth,
was presently lightened by the discharge of
ballast, and rose to a height of 12,000 feet into
the air. Immediately afterwards, when all
around was wrapped in the deepest silence
and the blackest darkness, there came the
sound of a sharp explosion from over their
heads, followed by a rustling of the silk, and
immediately the car received a violent jerk.
The same thing was repeated again and yet
again, and it is small wonder that the awful
conviction then seized the party that there, in
the darkness, in the dead of night, at that
fearful height, their balloon had burst, and
they were falling headlong to the ground.
Great indeed must have been their relief
when they found this was not the case, and
discovered the real reason of their alarm.

It is the tendency of a balloon when flying

near the ground to assume an elongated or pear shape; and while their balloon was in this position the netting, which was wet with dew, had frozen hard and tight around it. Immediately they rose to great heights the gas had expanded, and the balloon had become globular in shape, with a result that the stiffened ropes sprang to their new position with the crack and jerk which had so startled the party. When day broke next morning they found themselves over long tracts of desolate forest land, and fearing they were approaching the wild, inhospitable steppes of Russia, they descended with all speed, and discovered they were in the Duchy of Nassau, in Germany, near Weilburg, where they were received with the wildest enthusiasm and delight. From start to finish they had accomplished a voyage of 500 miles in eighteen hours.

After this event Green made many other voyages in the great Nassau balloon, and met with many exciting adventures. On one occasion, ascending in a violent gale of wind, he and a passenger covered twenty miles in a quarter of an hour, and, on descending near Rainham, in Essex, were blown along across the fields at a furious pace, until the anchor caught, and brought them up with such a wrench that it broke the ring and jerked the car completely upside down. Green and his friend only escaped from being thrown out by

D

holding on to the ropes, and they were afterwards dragged wildly through fences and
hedges until the balloon collapsed and came
to a stand, though not before they had both
been severely hurt.

On another voyage the famous balloon met
with serious injury, for having been some time
above the clouds, during an ascent, Green
found himself carried out to sea, and was
obliged to come down in the water two miles
north of Sheerness.   As in the accident which
befell Mr. Sadler in his attempt to cross the
Irish Channel, the wind caught the silk and
bore it along across the water too rapidly for
a pursuing vessel to overtake it.   Green then
lowered his anchor, which by happy chance
soon became entangled in a sunken wreck,
and so brought the balloon up.   A boat immediately put out to his assistance, and he
and a companion were speedily rescued; but
the balloon was so restive in the wind that
it was dangerous to approach it.   Green himself then suggested that a volley of musketry
should be fired into the silk to expel the gas,
and this was accordingly done and the balloon
secured, though it afterwards took Green a
fortnight's hard labour to repair the damage
done to the fabric.

But the saddest event connected with the
Nassau balloon was the fatal accident which
befell Mr. Cocking in 1837, the year after the
great Nassau voyage.   Before relating this,

however, it will be necessary to refer briefly to the history of a most important accessory of the balloon, hitherto unmentioned — the parachute.

The name parachute comes from two French words, *parer*, to parry and *chute*, a fall, and it signifies a contrivance, made more or less in the form of an enormous umbrella, to break the fall from a balloon or other great height. The principle of the parachute was understood even before the invention of the balloon. In Eastern countries, in particular, where the umbrella or parasol has been in familiar use from earliest ages, parachutes were frequently employed by acrobats to enable them to jump safely from great elevations. In France also, at the end of the eighteenth century, a captive officer attempted to escape from a lofty prison by similar means.

The aeronaut Blanchard was the first to construct a parachute for use from a balloon, his idea being that it might prove of service in the event of an accident while aloft. In 1785 he let down from a great height a parachute to which was attached a dog in a basket, which reached the ground gently and safely. After this M. Garnerin, the famous balloonist already referred to, hazarded a parachute descent in person, and his attempt being eminently satisfactory, parachute descents became fairly common.

In August 1814 Mr. Cocking, an English

gentleman of scientific tastes, read a paper on parachutes, suggesting an amendment in their shape and construction, before the Society of Arts, for which he was awarded a medal. His theory was never put into practice, however, till twenty-three years later, when, fired no doubt by the interest aroused by the famous Nassau voyage, he resolved to put his invention to the test.

He accordingly constructed his parachute, which was of enormous size, of unwieldy weight, and in shape rather resembling an umbrella turned inside out. Despite the warning of friends that the untried machine was unwisely built, he insisted on making a descent with it, and succeeded in persuading Mr. Green to take him and his craft aloft attached to the Nassau balloon.

On the 27th of July 1837 they started from the Vauxhall Gardens, Mr. Green in the car accompanied by Mr. Edward Spencer (grandfather of the present well-known firm of aeronauts), his friend and frequent companion ; Mr. Cocking seated in his machine slung below. A height of 5000 feet was attained, and then Mr. Cocking, after bidding a hearty farewell to the others, pulled the rope which liberated his parachute from the balloon. Relieved from the enormous weight, the latter rushed upwards into the sky with terrific velocity, the gas pouring in volumes from the valves and almost suffocating the occupants of

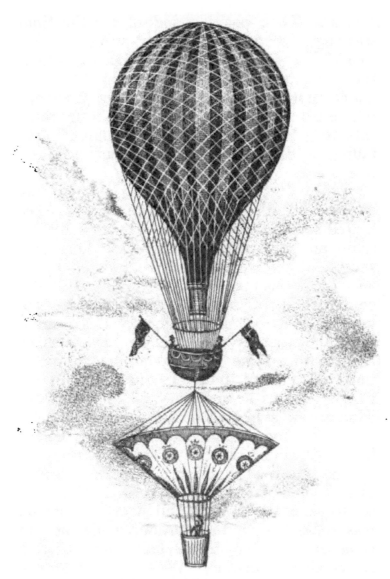

COCKING'S PARACHUTE.

the car. Their position, indeed, for the time was one of the greatest danger, and they were thankful to reach the earth unharmed, which they eventually did. But their fate was happier far than that of the luckless Cocking, whose parachute, after swaying fearfully from side to side, at length utterly collapsed, and falling headlong, was, with its inventor, dashed to pieces.

While Charles Green was making his famous ascents in England, an equally celebrated aeronaut, John Wise, was pursuing the same art in America. During a long and successful career, unhappily terminated by an accident, Wise made many experiments in the construction of balloons, their shape, size, varnish, material, and so forth. His results, which he carefully put together, have been of the greatest value to balloon manufacturers until the present time. In the course of his many voyages he met with various exciting adventures. On one occasion while aloft he saw before him a huge black cloud of particularly forbidding aspect. Entering this, he found himself in the heart of a terrific storm. His balloon was caught in a whirlwind, and set so violently spinning and swinging that he was sea-sick with the motion, while, at the same time, he felt himself half-suffocated and scarce able to breathe. Within the cloud the cold was intense; the ropes of the balloon became glazed with ice and snow till they resembled glass rods; hail fell around, and the gloom was so great that from the car the silk above became invisible. " A noise resembling the rushing of a thousand mill-dams, intermingled with a dismal moaning sound of wind, surrounded me in this terrible flight." Wise adds, " Bright sunshine was just above the clouds ; " but though he endeavoured to reach it by throwing out ballast, the balloon had no sooner begun to rise upwards than it was caught afresh by the storm and whirled down again. Neither was he able, by letting out gas, to escape this furious vortex from beneath; and for twenty minutes he was swept to and fro, and up and down in the cloud, before he could get clear of it, or regain any control over his balloon.

On another occasion Wise made an exceedingly daring and bold experiment. Convinced of the power which, as has before been said, an empty balloon has of turning itself into a natural parachute, he determined to put the matter to the test, and deliberately to burst his balloon when at a great height. For this purpose he made a special balloon of very thin material, and fastened up the neck so that there was no vent for the gas. He then ascended fearlessly to a height of 13,000 feet, where, through the expansion of the hydrogen with which it was filled, his balloon exploded. The gas escaped instantly, so that in ten seconds not a trace remained. The empty balloon at first descended with fearful rapidity, with a strange moaning sound as the air rushed through the network. Then the silk assuming parachute shape, the fall became less rapid, and finally the car, coming down in zigzags, turned upside down when close to the ground, and tossed Wise out into a field unhurt.

It was John Wise's great desire at one time to sail a balloon right across the Atlantic from America to Europe. Long study of the upper winds had convinced him that a regular current of air is always blowing steadily high aloft from west to east, and he believed that if an aeronaut could only keep his balloon in this upper current he might be carried across the ocean quicker, and with more ease and safety, than in the fastest steamship. Wise went so far as to work out all the details for this plan, the size of the balloon required, the ballast, provisions, and number of passengers; and only the want of sufficient money prevented him from actually making the attempt. Curiously enough, about the same time, Charles Green, in England, was, quite independently, working at the same idea, which he also believed, with proper equipment, to be quite feasible.

CHAPTER IV

THE BALLOON AS A SCIENTIFIC INSTRUMENT

So far, in our history of aeronautics, we have referred to ballooning only as a sport or pastime for the amusement of spectators, and for the gratifying of a love of adventure. It is now time to speak of the practical uses of the balloon, and how it has been employed as a most valuable scientific instrument to teach us facts about the upper atmosphere, its nature and extent, the clouds, the winds and their ways, the travel of sounds, and many other things of which we should otherwise be ignorant.

Before the invention of the balloon men were quite unaware of the nature of the air even a short distance above their heads. In those days high mountain climbing had not come into fashion, and when Pilâtre de Rozier made the first ascent, it was considered very doubtful whether he might be able to exist in the strange atmosphere aloft. Charles and Roberts were the first to make scientific observations from a balloon, for they took up a thermometer and barometer, and made certain rough records, as also did other early aeronauts. The most interesting purely scien-

tific ascents of early days, however, were made
in the autumn of 1804, from Paris, by Gay
Lussac, a famous French philosopher. He
took up with him all manner of instruments,
among them a compass (to see if the needle
behaved the same as on earth), an apparatus to
test the electricity of the air, thermometers,
barometers, and hygrometers, carefully exhausted flasks in which to bring down samples
of the upper air, birds, and even insects and
frogs, to see how great heights affected them.
In his second voyage his balloon attained the
enormous altitude of 23,000 feet, or more than
four miles and a quarter, and nearly 2000 feet
higher than the highest peaks of the Andes.
At this tremendous height the temperature
fell to far below freezing-point, and the aeronaut became extremely cold, though warmly
clad; he also felt headache, a difficulty in
breathing, and his throat became so parched
that he could hardly swallow. Nevertheless,
undismayed by the awfulness of his position,
he continued making his observations, and
eventually reached the ground in safety, and
none the worse for his experience.

Gay Lussac's experiments at least proved
that though the air becomes less and less dense
as we ascend into it, it remains of the same
nature and constitution. His second voyage
also showed that the limit to which man
could ascend aloft into the sky and yet live
had not yet been reached. Almost sixty

years later other scientific ascents threw fresh
light on this point, and also continued the
other investigations that Gay Lussac had
commenced.

Towards the close of Charles Green's famous
career, scientific men in England woke up to
the fact that the use of a balloon as an important means for obtaining observations on
meteorology and other matters had of late
been very much neglected. The British Association took the matter up, and provided
the money for four scientific ascents, which
were made by Mr. Welsh of Kew Observatory, a trained observer. Green was the
aeronaut chosen to accompany him, and the
balloon used was none other than the great
Nassau balloon, of whose many and wonderful adventures we have already spoken. Green
was then nearly seventy years of age, but his
skill as an aeronaut was as great as ever, and
Welsh was able to obtain many valuable
records. During the last voyage a height was
attained almost as great as that reached by
Gay Lussac, and both men found much difficulty in breathing. While at this elevation
they suddenly noticed they were rapidly approaching the sea, and so were forced to make
a very hasty descent, in which many of the
instruments were broken.

The veteran Green lived to a ripe old age,
dying in 1870, aged eighty-five. When a very
old man he still delighted in taking visitors to

an outhouse where he kept the old Nassau balloon, now worn out and useless, and, handling it affectionately, would talk of its famous adventures and his own thousand ascents, during which he had never once met with serious accident or failure. After his death the old balloon passed into the hands of another equally famous man, who, after Green's retirement, took his place as the most celebrated English aeronaut of the day.

This was Henry Coxwell. He was the son of a naval officer, and was brought up to the profession of a dentist. But when a boy of only nine years old he watched, through his father's telescope, a balloon ascent by Green, which so fired his imagination that henceforward balloons filled all his thoughts. As he grew older the fascination increased upon him. He would go long distances to see ascents or catch glimpses of balloons in the air, and he was fortunate enough to be present at the first launching of the great Nassau balloon. He did not get the chance of a voyage aloft, however, till he was twenty-five; but after this nothing could restrain his ardour, and, throwing his profession to the winds, he made ascent after ascent on all possible occasions.

In one of his early voyages he met with what he describes as one of the most perilous descents in the whole history of ballooning. The occasion was an evening ascent made from the

Vauxhall Gardens one autumn night of 1848.
The aeronaut was a Mr. Gypson, and besides
Mr. Coxwell there were two other passengers,
one of whom was the well-known mountaineer
and lecturer, Albert Smith. A number of
fireworks which were to be displayed when

COXWELL.   GLAISHER.

aloft were slung on a framework forty feet
below the car.

The balloon rose high above London, and
the party were amazed and delighted with the
strange and lovely view of the great city by
night, all sight of the houses being lost in the
darkness, and the thousands of gas lamps, out-
lining the invisible streets and bridges, twink-

ling like stars in a blue-black sky. Coxwell
was sitting, not in the car, but in the ring of
the balloon, and presently, when they were
about 7000 feet above the town, he noticed that
the silk, the mouth of which appears to have
been fastened, was growing dangerously dis-
tended with the expanding gas. By his advice
the valve was immediately pulled, but it was
already too late; the balloon burst, the gas
escaped with a noise like the escape of steam
from an engine, the silk collapsed, and the
balloon began to descend with appalling
speed, the immense mass of loose silk surging
and rustling frightfully overhead. Everything
was immediately thrown out of the car to
break the fall; but the wind still seemed to
be rushing past at a fearful rate, and, to add
to the horror of the aeronauts, they now came
down through the remains of the discharged
fireworks floating in the air. Little bits of
burning cases and still smouldering touch-
paper blew about them, and were caught in
the rigging. These kindled into sparks, and
there seemed every chance of the whole balloon
catching alight. They were still a whole mile
from the ground, and this distance they appear
to have covered in less than two minutes.
The house-tops seemed advancing up towards
them with awful speed as they neared earth.
In the end they were tossed out of the car
along the ground, and it appeared a perfect
marvel to them all that they escaped with only

a severe shaking. This adventure did not in the least abate Coxwell's ardour for ballooning, and exactly a week later he and Gypson successfully made the same ascent from the same place, and in the same balloon—and loaded with twice the number of fireworks !

But Coxwell's most celebrated voyage of all took place some years later, on the occasion of a scientific voyage made in company with Mr. James Glaisher.   In 1862 the British Association determined to continue the balloon observations which Mr. Welsh had so successfully commenced, but this time on a larger scale.   The observer was to be Mr. Glaisher of Greenwich Observatory, and Mr. Coxwell, who by this time had become a recognised aeronaut, undertook the management of the balloon.   The first ascents were made in July and August.   Mr. Glaisher took up a most elaborate and costly outfit of instruments, which, however, were badly damaged at the outset during a very rapid descent, made perforce to avoid falling in the " Wash."   On each occasion a height of over four miles was attained ; but on the third voyage, which was in September, it was decided to try and reach yet greater altitudes.

The balloon with its two passengers left Wolverhampton at 1 P.M.—the temperature on the ground being 59°.   At about a mile high a dense cloud was entered, and the thermometer fell to 36°.   In nineteen minutes a height of two miles was reached, and the air was at freezing-point. Six minutes later they were three miles aloft, with the thermometer still falling; and by the time four miles high was attained the mercury registered only 8°.

In forty-seven minutes from the start five miles had been passed; and now the temperature was 2° below zero. Mr. Coxwell, who was up in the ring of the balloon and exerting himself over the management of it, found he was beginning to breathe with great difficulty. Mr. Glaisher, sitting quietly in the car watching his instruments, felt no inconvenience. More ballast was thrown out, and the balloon continued to rise apace; and soon Mr. Glaisher found his eyes growing strangely dim. He could not see to read his thermometer, or distinguish the hands of his watch. He noticed the mercury of the barometer, however, and saw that a height of 29,000 feet had been reached, and the balloon was still rising. What followed next had best be told in Mr. Glaisher's own words :—

"Shortly after I laid my arm upon the table, possessed of its full vigour, but on being desirous of using it, I found it useless. Trying to move the other arm, I found it powerless also. Then I tried to shake myself and succeeded, but I seemed to have no limbs. In looking at the barometer my head fell over my left shoulder. I struggled and shook my body again, but could not move my arms.

Getting my head upright for an instant only, it fell on my right shoulder; then I fell backwards, my body resting against the side of the car, and my head on the edge.   I dimly saw Mr. Coxwell and endeavoured to speak, but could not.   In an instant intense darkness overcame me; but I was still conscious, with as active a brain as at the present moment while writing this.   I thought I had been seized with asphyxia, and believed I should experience nothing more, as death would come unless we speedily descended.   Other thoughts were entering my mind, when I suddenly became unconscious as on going to sleep."   Mr. Glaisher adds: " I cannot tell anything of the sense of hearing, as no sound reaches the ear to break the perfect stillness and silence of the regions between six and seven miles above the earth."

Meanwhile, as stated, Mr. Coxwell was up in the ring, trying to secure the valve-line, which had become twisted.   To do this he had taken off a pair of thick gloves he had been wearing, and in the tremendous cold of that awful region the moment his bare hands rested on the metal of the ring they became frost-bitten and useless.   Looking down, he saw Mr. Glaisher in a fainting condition, and called out to him, but received no answer. Thoroughly alarmed by this time, he tried to come down to his companion's assistance; but now *his* hands also had become lifeless, and

E

he felt unconsciousness rapidly stealing over him.

Quickly realising that death to both of them would speedily follow if the balloon continued to ascend, Mr. Coxwell now endeavoured to pull the valve-line ; but he found it impossible to do so with his disabled hands. Fortunately he was a man of great bodily strength, as well as of iron nerve, and by a great effort he succeeded in catching the valve-line *in his teeth*. Then, putting his whole weight upon it, he managed to pull open the valve, and hold it until the balloon took a decided turn downwards. This saved them. As lower regions were reached, where the air was denser, Mr. Glaisher began to recover, and by the time they came to the ground neither of these two brave men were any the worse for their extraordinary experience.

Neither Mr. Glaisher or Mr. Coxwell were able to note the exact elevation when they were at their greatest height ; but from several circumstances they were convinced that it must have been 36,000 or 37,000 feet, or fully *seven miles high*. Later aeronauts have been inclined to doubt if this surmise can be quite correct ; but whether it is so or not is of no great moment, for this great balloon ascent will always stand unrivalled in the history of ballooning. Since that day nearly as great, or perhaps even greater, heights have been reached in balloons; but nowadays those who attempt to ascend to great elevations always provide themselves, before they start, with cylinders of compressed oxygen gas. Then when the atmosphere aloft becomes so thin and rare as to make breathing difficult, they begin to fill their lungs with the life-giving gas from the cylinders, and at once recover.

After this perilous voyage Glaisher and Coxwell made several other scientific balloon ascents. They met with various experiences. On one occasion, during a lofty ascent, they lost sight of the earth above the clouds for a while, but, the mist suddenly breaking, they found themselves on the point of drifting out to sea. Not a moment was to be lost, and both men hung on to the valve-line until it cut their hands. The result was a tremendously rapid descent. The balloon fell four and a quarter miles in less than a quarter of an hour, covering the last two miles in only four minutes. They reached earth close to the shore, and were fortunate to escape with only a few bruises, though all the instruments were once more broken in the shock.

Mr. Glaisher was able to make many interesting notes of the condition of the winds and clouds at high levels. He observed how frequently different currents of air are blowing aloft in different directions at the same time. These differing winds

affect the shape of the clouds among which
they blow.   High above the ground he
frequently met with a warm wind blowing
constantly from the south-west; and he believed that it is largely due to this mild air-
stream passing always overhead that England
enjoys such much less rigorous winters than
other countries that lie as far north of the
equator.   This mildness of our climate has
long been attributed to the Gulf Stream,
that warm current of the sea which sweeps
up from the tropics past our shores.   But it
may well be that there is besides an " Aerial
Gulf Stream," as Mr. Glaisher calls it, blowing
constantly above our heads, which also serves
to warm the air, and make our winter climate
mild and moist.

One fact these experiments seemed to
establish was, that when rain is falling from
an overcast sky, there is always a higher layer
of clouds overhanging the lower stratum.
Nothing surprised Mr. Glaisher more than
the extreme rapidity with which the whole
sky, up to a vast height, could fill up entirely
with clouds at the approach of a storm.
Another point noted was that, when a wind
is blowing, the upper portion of the current
always travels faster than that next the
ground.   This is due, of course, to the
obstacles the wind meets as it sweeps over
the earth, and which check its onward
progress.

These, and very many other facts of the greatest interest to the meteorologist, were the outcome of Mr. Glaisher's experiments. Later voyages of a similar kind have added greatly to our knowledge of the condition of the air, and it seems certain that in the future the balloon will be much more used by scientific men, and by its means they will be able to predict the weather more accurately and further ahead than at present, and learn many other things of which we are now in ignorance.

CHAPTER V

THE BALLOON IN WARFARE

But there is another practical use for the balloon to which we must now refer, and that a most important one—its employment in war-time. It was not long after the invention of this ship of the skies that soldiers began to realise what a valuable aid it might be to them in times of battle, enabling them to see inside a camp, fort, or beleaguered city, or watch the enemy's movements from afar off. The opportunity for first putting the matter to the test very soon arose. Within a very few years of the earliest balloon experiments in France there commenced

in that very country the dreadful French
Revolution, and soon the nation found itself
at war with all the world, and forced to hold
its own, alone, against the armies of Europe.
This danger quickened the minds of all to
the importance of making use of every possible means of defence in their power.   It
was suggested that the newly discovered
balloon might be turned to account, and
immediately a school for military ballooning
was established near Paris.   Fifty young
military students were trained in the new
art, and suitable balloons were provided.
The value of their work was soon apparent.
In June 1794 was fought the battle of
Fleurus, between the French and Austrians.
Before the fight a balloon party had carefully
observed the position of the Austrian forces,
and, through the information they gave, the
French were able to gain a speedy and de-
cisive victory.   In this way, and at this early
stage, the value of the war balloon was at
once established.

Curiously enough, Napoleon would make
no use of balloons in his campaigns, and even
did away with the balloon school at Paris.
The reason given for his prejudice is a curious
one.   At the time of his coronation a large,
unmanned balloon, gaily decorated, and carrying thousands of lights, was sent up from
Paris during the evening's illuminations.   It
was a very beautiful object, and behaved

splendidly, sailing away into the night, amidst great popular rejoicing, until it was lost to sight in the darkness. But at daybreak next morning it was seen approaching the city of Rome, where it presently arrived, actually hovering over St. Peter's and the Vatican. Then, as if its mission were fulfilled, it settled to earth, and finally fell in Lake Bracciano. But as it fell it rent itself, and left a portion of the crown with which it was ornamented on the tomb of the Roman Emperor Nero. Napoleon, who was always a superstitious man, saw in this extraordinary voyage some dreadful forecast of his own fate. He was much disturbed, and forebade the matter ever to be mentioned in his presence ; nor would he henceforward have any more to do with balloons.

Military balloons were used by the French again, however, during their war in Africa in 1880. The Austrians also used them in 1849, and it is said the Russians had them at the siege of Sebastopol in the Crimean War. A Montgolfier balloon was made use of by the French in 1862 at the battle of Solferino; and the Americans also employed balloons during the Civil War a year later. The American war balloons were comparatively small ones, inflated with hydrogen. The hydrogen was manufactured in the way already described, by pouring dilute sulphuric acid upon scrap-iron. For making the gas upon the field two large tanks of wood called "generators" were used. In these the water and scrap-iron were placed and the acid poured upon them, the gas produced being carried to the balloon through pipes, passing first

AMERICAN WAR BALLOON.

through vessels filled with lime-water to cool and purify it. When on the march four waggons were sufficient to carry the whole apparatus. The inflation, which took some time, was made as close to the scene of action as was considered safe, and when the balloon was once full a party of men could easily tow it about to where it was needed.

But the time when the balloon was most largely and most usefully used in time of war was during the Siege of Paris. In the month of September 1870, during the Franco-Prussian War, Paris was closely invested by the Prussian forces, and for eighteen long weeks lay besieged and cut off from all the rest of the world. No communication with the city was possible either by road, river, rail, or telegraph, nor could the inhabitants convey tidings of their plight save by one means alone. Only the passage of the air was open to them.

Quite at the beginning of the siege it occurred to the Parisians that they might use balloons to escape from the beleaguered town, and pass over the heads of the enemy to safety beyond; and inquiry was at once made to discover what aeronautical resources were at their command.

It was soon found that with only one or two exceptions the balloons actually in existence within the walls were unserviceable or unsuitable for the work on hand, being mostly old ones which had been laid aside as worthless. One lucky discovery was, however, made. Two professional aeronauts, of well-proved experience and skill, were in Paris at the time. These were MM. Godard and Yon, both of whom had been in London only a short time before in connection with a huge captive balloon which was then being exhibited there. They at once received orders to establish two balloon factories, and begin making a large number of balloons as· quickly as possible. For their workshops they were given the use of two great railway stations, then standing idle and deserted. No better places for the purpose could be imagined, for under the great glass roofs there was plenty of space, and the work went on apace.

As the balloons were intended to make only one journey each, plain white or coloured calico (of which there was plenty in the city), covered with quick-drying varnish, was considered good enough for their material. Hundreds of men and women were employed at the two factories; and altogether some sixty balloons were turned out during the siege. Their management was entrusted to sailors, who, of all men, seemed most fitted for the work. The only previous training that could be given them was to sling them up to the roof of the railway stations in a balloon car, and there make them go through the actions of throwing out ballast, dropping the anchor, and pulling the valve-line. This was, of course, very like learning to swim on dry land; nevertheless, these amateurs made, on the whole, very fair aeronauts.

But before the first of the new balloons was ready experiments were already being made with the few old balloons then in Paris. Two were moored captive at different ends of the town to act as observation stations from whence the enemy's movements could be watched. Captive ascents were made in them every few hours. Meanwhile M. Duruof, a professional aeronaut, made his escape from the city in an old and unskyworthy balloon called "Le Neptune," descending safely outside the enemy's lines, while another equally successful voyage was made with two small balloons fastened together.

And then, as soon as the possibility of leaving Paris by this means was fully proved, an important new development arose. So far, as was shown, tidings of the besieged city could be conveyed to the outside world; but how was news from without to reach those imprisoned within? The problem was presently solved in a most ingenious way.

There was in Paris, when the siege commenced, a society or club of pigeon-fanciers who were specially interested in the breeding and training of "carrier" or "homing" pigeons. The leaders of this club now came forward and suggested to the authorities that, with the aid of the balloons, their birds might be turned to practical account as letter-carriers. The idea was at once taken up, and henceforward every balloon that sailed out of Paris contained not only letters and despatches, but also a number of properly trained pigeons, which, when liberated, would find their way back to their homes within the walls of the besieged city.

When the pigeons had been safely brought out of Paris, and fallen into friendly hands beyond the Prussian forces, there were attached to the tail feathers of each of them goose quills, about two inches long, fastened on by a silken thread or thin wire. Inside these were tiny scraps of photographic film, not much larger than postage stamps, upon which a large number of messages had been photographed by microscopic photography. So skilfully was this done that each scrap of film could contain 2500 messages of twenty words each. A bird might easily carry a dozen of these films, for the weight was always less than one gramme, or 15½ grains. One bird, in fact, arrived in Paris on the 3rd of February carrying eighteen films, containing altogether 40,000 messages. To avoid accidents, several copies of the same film were made, and attached to different birds. When any of the pigeons arrived in Paris their despatches were enlarged and thrown on a screen by a magic-lantern, then copied and sent to those for whom they were intended.

This system of balloon and pigeon post went on during the whole siege. Between sixty and seventy balloons left the city, carrying altogether nearly 200 people, and two and a half million letters, weighing in all about ten tons. The greater number of these arrived in safety, while the return journeys, accomplished by the birds, were scarcely less successful. The weather was very unfavourable during most of the time, and cold and fogs prevented many pigeons from making their way back to Paris. Of 360 birds brought safely out of the city by balloon only about 60 returned, but these had carried between them some 100,000 messages.

Of the balloons themselves two, each with its luckless aeronaut, were blown out to sea and never heard of more. Two sailed into Germany and were captured by the enemy, three more came down too soon and fell into the hands of the besieging army near Paris, and one did not even get as far as the Prussian lines. Others experienced accidents and rough landings in which their passengers were more or less injured. Moreover, each balloon which sailed by day from the city became at once a mark for the enemy's fire; so much so that before long it became necessary to make all the ascents by night, under cover of darkness.

They were brave men indeed who dared face the perils of a night voyage in an untried balloon, manned by an unskilled pilot, and exposed to the fire of the enemy, into whose hands they ran the greatest risk of falling. It is small wonder there was much excitement in Paris when it became known that the first of the new balloons made during

the siege was to take away no less a personage
than M. Gambetta, the great statesman, who
was at the time, and for long after, the leading
man in France.   He made his escape by
balloon on the 7th of October, accompanied
by his secretary and an aeronaut, and managed to reach a safe haven, though not before
they had been vigorously fired at by shot
and shell, and M. Gambetta himself had
actually been grazed on the hand by a
bullet.

Another distinguished man who hazarded the
same perilous feat, though for a very different
reason, was M. Janssen, a famous astronomer.
On the 22nd of December of that year there
was to take place an important total eclipse
of the sun, which would be visible in Spain
and Algeria.   It had long been M. Janssen's
intention to observe this eclipse, and for this
purpose he had prepared a special telescope
and apparatus; but when the time drew near
he found himself and his instruments shut up
in besieged Paris, with no possible means of
escape except the dangerous and desperate
hazard of a voyage by sky.

But so great was the astronomer's enthusiasm for his work, that he resolved to
brave even this risk.   Taking the essential
parts of his telescope with him, and, as aeronaut, an active young sailor, he set sail in
the darkness of a winter's morning, long
before dawn, passed safely over the enemy's

lines, and continued the voyage till nearly mid-day, when they sighted the sea, and came down near the mouth of the river Loire, having travelled 800 miles in little more than five hours. Neither Janssen or his telescope were injured in the descent, though the wind was high at the time; and both reached Algeria in time for the eclipse. It must have been a most bitter disappointment to the ardent astronomer, after all his exertions, that when the great day arrived the sun was hidden by clouds, and he was unable to observe the sight for which he had risked so much.

Since the Franco-Prussian war, military ballooning has been largely developed, and now all great armies possess their properly equipped and trained balloon corps. The balloons in use in the British Army at the present day are made, not of silk, but of gold-beater's skin, a very thin, but extremely tough membrane prepared from the insides of oxen. This is, of course, much stronger and more durable than ordinary balloon fabric, but much more expensive. The balloons are comparatively small ones, of 10,000 feet capacity, and are inflated with hydrogen. The hydrogen is now no longer made upon the field, but is manufactured in special factories, and carried compressed in large steel cylinders. By this means the time occupied in filling the balloon is much reduced, but the weight of the cylinders is very great. As will be remembered, balloons were made of considerable use during the late Boer War. At the siege of Ladysmith they were thought of much value in directing the fire of the British Artillery, and again at Spion Kop and Magersfontein are said to have done good service.

So far we have shown of what use balloons may be in times of peace and war. Every year sees fresh improvements and developments in balloons for military purposes and in those employed for making meteorological and other similar observations; and there is no doubt that great advances may shortly be expected in both these directions. But there is yet another and totally different science to which the balloon may lend its aid, and help greatly to add to our knowledge; and this is the science of geography, or the study of the earth's surface.

One of the earliest ideas suggested by Montgolfier's invention was that the balloon might be turned to practical account in the exploring of unknown and inaccessible tracts of the world. It was suggested that in a balloon men might sail over and survey country that they were not able to reach in any other way. Deserts could be crossed in this fashion, forests and mountain ranges, and even the desolate ice-tracts of the North and South Poles.

All this is, in truth, perfectly possible, and another day may be accomplished; but at

present great difficulties and dangers stand in
the way of exploring by balloon, and up to
the present time, with one great exception,
no special attempt has been made. It has
already been mentioned that both Wise and
Green wished to cross the Atlantic by sky,
and indeed at the present moment plans are
actually being made on the Continent for a
similar voyage. This, however, can scarcely
be called exploring. Other suggestions
which may presently be put to the test
are the crossing of the Sahara, and also of
another great desert in Central Arabia, into
which no white man has ever succeeded in
penetrating. Recent expeditions both to the
North and South Poles have also taken with
them balloons to be used captive for the
observation of the state of the ice ahead,
and for obtaining wide views around.

The one great attempt at exploring by
balloon which has so far been made has, unfortunately, met with hopeless and terrible
disaster—this was the ill-fated voyage to the
North Pole of Andrée and his companions.
The idea of reaching the Pole by balloon
was first proposed many years ago, and both
French and English aeronauts at different
times have made suggestions as to the best
way in which it might be accomplished.
Nothing, however, was attempted until about
the year 1894, when M. S. A. Andrée, a well-
known Swedish balloonist, who had already

F

met with exciting experiences in the air, made
up his mind actually to risk the venture.

His plan was to take a suitable balloon, and
the apparatus for inflating it, to a place as far
north as a ship could safely go, then to fill
the balloon and wait for a favourable wind
which should carry him right over the Pole and
beyond until inhabited country was reached.
By the summer of 1896 all his preparations
were complete. His balloon was an enormous
one, capable of holding 162,000 cubic feet of
gas, and was fitted with a rudder sail and a
long trail-rope, by means of which Andrée
hoped to be able to some extent to steer his
course across the ice. Two companions were
to accompany him on his voyage, and on June
7th the party embarked with all their apparatus, and were conveyed to Spitzbergen.

They landed at Dane's Island, where their
first work was to build themselves a shed.
They then got their gas-making apparatus
into order, and filled the balloon, and by the
27th of July were all ready for a start. But
the wind was contrary, and day after day they
waited in vain for a change, until at last the
captain of the ship which had brought them
warned them they would be frozen in for the
winter unless they returned without delay.
Very reluctantly, therefore, they abandoned
their venture for that year, and went home,
leaving behind them the shed and gas-gener-
ator for another occasion.

The winter passed, and by the end of next May they were back again at Dane's Island. Their shed and apparatus had suffered damage during their absence, and had to be repaired, and their preparations were not complete until the end of June. But again the wind was contrary, and for three weeks more they waited impatiently. All this while the balloon remained inflated, and by the long delay must have lost a considerable amount of its buoyancy. At last the wind changed, and though it was not exactly in the direction they wished, being a little west of south, instead of due south, Andrée felt he could wait no longer, and at half-past two in the afternoon of July 11th set sail, with his two friends, on his daring voyage.

What followed is soon told. Eleven days later one of the carrier pigeons taken by Andrée in his balloon was picked up by a fishing-boat off Spitzbergen. Fastened to it was the following message: — "July 13th, 12.30 P.M. 82° 2′ north lat., 15° 5′ east long. Good journey eastward. All goes well on board.—ANDRÉE."

This was the latest news ever heard of the ill-fated voyagers. Later on two of Andrée's buoys, thrown ·out from the balloon, were found; but the messages these contained were dated on the evening of July 11th, only a few hours after the start. If the date of the first found message can be relied on, it would seem that after forty-eight hours Andrée's balloon was still sailing well, and he had already accomplished the longest voyage aloft ever made.

Of his subsequent fate, and that of his companions, nothing is known. Search expeditions have failed to find any trace of them or of the balloon, and the many rumours received have been proved to be false. There can be no possible reason to doubt that these brave men perished in their daring attempt, and that their bones lie in the Arctic Sea or in the waste of ice and snow that surrounds the Pole.

CHAPTER VI

THE AIRSHIP

So far in our story we have traced the origin and progress of the balloon, showing how from small beginnings it has grown to be an important invention, of great use to the scientific observer, the soldier, and the explorer, and the means of teaching us much fresh knowledge.

But in spite of the high hopes of early aeronauts, and the extravagant prophecies made when the first balloons ascended into the sky, it has long been evident that the balloon alone has not solved the problem of human flight or accomplished the conquest of the air. An ordinary balloon is, in fact, nothing more than a mere lifting machine, no more capable of sailing the sky, in the proper sense of the word, than a cork floating in the water is capable of sailing the sea. It has no movement of its own, but drifts simply at the mercy of the wind, and quite beyond control. By the discharge of ballast, or by the letting out of gas, the aeronaut can indeed cause it to rise or sink at pleasure, and sometimes when two currents of air are blowing aloft in different directions at the same time he may, by passing from one to the other, "tack" his balloon to some extent across the sky. Otherwise he has no power of guiding or directing it in the least degree, and should he lose sight of the earth above the clouds, has even no method of telling in which direction he is travelling.

Early inventors thought they would be able to steer balloons by means of sails, like a boat, but they soon found that this was impossible. The effect of hoisting a sail at the side of a balloon was merely to swing the balloon round until the sail was in front, while meantime it continued its course unaltered. The use of a rudder and other means were also tried, but without success ; nor can such methods ever hope to succeed so long as a balloon floats in the air at the same pace as the wind that carries it forward. A balloon travelling with the wind may be compared

to a boat drifting idly with the tide. As
long as she drifts she refuses to answer her
rudder, which swings idly. But presently the
boatman hoists a sail, and the wind carries the
boat onwards faster than the tide, and then
immediately the rudder comes into action.
Or should there be no wind, he may accomplish the same thing by dragging an anchor
or other weight in the water, and so slowing
his boat down until it moves slower than
the current; he will then again find that his
boat will answer her helm.

To steer his course in a balloon, therefore,
the aeronaut must so arrange that he is
travelling faster or slower than the wind in
which he finds himself. To travel faster, he
must employ some sort of engine or motor
to drive his craft onwards. To travel slower,
he must trail something along the ground
beneath to act as a drag.

Part of the equipment of every balloon is
a long trail-rope, which, when the balloon
is aloft, hangs some 300 feet below the car.
The object of this rope is to break the force
of the fall when the balloon comes down to
the earth at the end of the voyage. In the
greater number of cases a balloon, in its final
swoop to the ground, falls the last few hundred
feet with considerable, and often uncomfortable, speed. But when provided with a trail-
rope, as it descends more and more of the
heavy rope will lie along the ground, and so

lighten the weight of the balloon, and lessen the shock of falling.

If then a trail-rope were used of such length that it would sweep along the ground while the balloon was flying in the air, the effect would be to put a drag or brake on the balloon, and so render it capable of being steered to some extent with a sail; and this is what has actually been done in all attempts of the kind. But since a long rope dragging rapidly across the country is a very dangerous object, capable of doing great damage, and also liable to catch in trees and other obstacles, such experiments can only be tried with safety over the sea, or, as in the case of Andrée's voyage, over desert or uninhabited country.

The best way of steering a balloon, therefore, is to provide it with some mechanical power which shall urge it onwards at a greater speed than the wind; and when this is done, it has ceased to be a balloon in the popular sense of the word, and has become an "airship."

There is a great deal of confusion between the terms "airship," and "flying machine," and the two words are often considered as meaning the same thing. But while, strictly speaking, neither word in itself has any very definite meaning, it is gradually becoming more general to apply them to two widely different objects. According to this plan, although both names stand for an aerial vessel capable of travelling in the sky by its own motion, an airship is a machine supported in the air by reason of its buoyancy, while a flying machine is kept aloft only by virtue of its onward movement.

In other words, part of the construction of an airship consists of a bag or balloon, filled with gas or hot air, which causes the whole to rise and maintain its position in the air. This balloon part is quite independent of the machinery which drives the airship forward, and indeed if the engine ceases working, the vessel becomes nothing more than an ordinary balloon in its nature, and will behave like one. An airship, therefore, is in principle an apparatus lighter than air.

A flying machine, on the contrary, is heavier than air, and maintains its position aloft merely by the power it obtains from its engines, assisted by its special construction. The inventors of flying machines take as their analogy the flight of birds. Birds are creatures heavier than air, which yet manage to rise and fly by reason of the strength and construction of their wings. In the same way the heavy flying machine essays to fly by the power of its machinery. And, as a bird aloft, if its wings became disabled, would instantly drop towards earth, so a flying machine would immediately commence to fall if its engine stopped or ceased to move with sufficient power. The airship and the flying machine, therefore, may be regarded as rival aerial vessels, and their inventors and advocates, sometimes known as "lighter-than-air-ites" and "heavier-than-air-ites," though both working for the same end, are endeavouring to accomplish their aim by widely different methods.

Up to the present day the airship—to which we will first turn our attention—has been much more largely and successfully experimented with than the flying machine. It is, however, the opinion of many, including the great authority Sir Hiram Maxim, that in the future the flying machine will become the more important invention of the two. "In all Nature," says Sir Hiram, "we do not find a single balloon. All Nature's flying machines are heavier than air." And from this he argues that, as Nature is ever our best guide and example, a flying machine heavier than air will be in the end most likely to succeed.

One of the earliest airships which achieved any success was invented by a Frenchman, M. Giffard, about the year 1852. He made his balloon of an elongated or cigar shape, a form adopted by airship inventors as offering less resistance to the air than the ordinary globular or pear shape. To this balloon, which was 104 feet long and 39 feet in diameter, he attached a steam-engine of three-horse power, weighing 462 lbs. and working a screw-propeller, which, by its rapid revolutions, urged the balloon onwards through the air, even as the screw of a steamship urges the vessel through the water. With this apparatus he succeeded on one occasion, for a very short while, in obtaining a speed of six and a half miles an hour. Twenty years later another Frenchman, M. Dupuy de Lôme, constructed another airship; but fearing to place an engine so near the gas of his balloon, he used the strength of eight men to work his screw. This was a very wasteful mode of supplying energy, for the weight of the men was very great in proportion to their strength, and this machine, during its trial, did not attain as great a speed as Giffard's. Twelve years after a third Frenchman, M. Tissandier, took up the same experiments. His elongated balloon was smaller than the two previous, and his engine was an electric motor of one and a half horse-power. On one occasion a speed of nearly eight miles an hour was attained.

By this time the French Government had become interested in the work, and provided money to continue investigations. The result of this was that in 1885 two officers of the French army, Captains Renard and Krebs, brought out by far the most successful airship yet constructed. It was 165 feet long, 27 feet in diameter, and was driven by an electric motor of nine horse-power. That this machine proved itself perfectly capable of being guided in the air is amply shown by the fact that it returned to its shed five times out of the seven on which it was publicly taken out. It also attained a speed of fourteen miles an hour, and indeed it would seem that Renard and Krebs, although their names are now almost forgotten, accomplished nearly as great things twenty years ago as the popular airship inventors of the present day.

One of the greatest difficulties with which early inventors had to contend was the enormous weight of their engines. The machinery they were obliged to use to drive their airships through the air weighed more than their balloons, unless made of unwieldy size, had power to lift. The same difficulty indeed exists at the present time, though to a much less degree. Of late years, and especially since the introduction of the motor-car, great progress has been made in the construction of light but powerful engines, or motors, and the employment of petrol vapour instead of coal or oil has very greatly lessened the weight of the fuel which has to be carried.

In consequence of this improvement many airships have recently been made which have met with varying success, and many more are at the present moment in process of construction. Among the host of inventors, whose names it would here be impossible even to mention, three stand out from the rest in special prominence—Zeppelin, Santos Dumont, and

Stanley Spencer — all three the inventors of airships which have, by actual experience, proved their power of steering a course across the sky.

Of these rival airships, by far the largest and most elaborate was that built by the first named, Count Zeppelin, a distinguished veteran soldier of the German army. For many years he had spent his time and fortune in making experiments in aerial navigation, and at length in 1900, having formed a company and collected a large sum of money for the purpose, he produced an enormous airship, which, from its size, has been compared to a man-of-war. In shape Count Zeppelin's invention resembled a gigantic cigar, 420 feet in length, pointed at both ends. The framework was made of the specially light metal aluminium, covered over with silk, and though from outside it looked all in one piece, within it was divided into seventeen compartments, each holding a separate balloon made of oiled silk and absolutely gas-tight. The object of this was to prevent the tendency the gas has to collect all at one end as the ship forces its way through the air. These balloons were filled with pure hydrogen, the cost of the inflation alone being £500. Beneath was slung a long gangway, 346 feet in length, with two cars, also made of aluminium, attached to it, In these cars were placed two motor-engines of sixteen horse-power each, driven by benzine, and working a pair of screw-propellers attached to the balloon. A steering apparatus was placed at each end, and the whole machine, with five passengers, weighed about eleven tons.

To lessen the effects of a possible fall, the

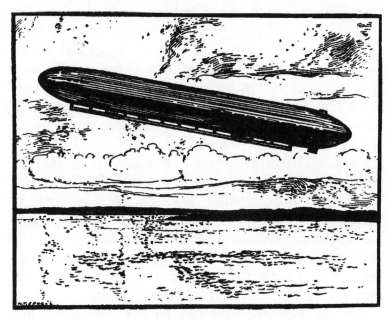

ZEPPELIN'S AIRSHIP OVER LAKE CONSTANCE.

experiments were carried out over water, and the great airship was housed in a shed built on Lake Constance. The cost of this shed alone was enormous, for it was elaborately constructed on pontoons, and anchored in such a way that it could be turned round to allow the airship to be liberated from it in the best direction to suit the wind.   The trial trip was made one evening in June 1900, when a very light wind was blowing.   The great machine rose into the air, carrying Zeppelin and four companions to a height of 800 feet.   The steering apparatus then being put into action, it circled round and faced the wind, remained stationary for a short while, and then sank gracefully and gently upon the water.   A few days later another and more successful trial was made.   The wind at the time was blowing at sixteen miles an hour, but in spite of this the airship slowly steered its course against the wind for three and a half miles, when, one of the rudders breaking, it was obliged to come down.   On one or two other occasions also it made successful voyages, proving itself to be perfectly manageable and capable of being steered on an absolutely calm day.   The expense of the experiments was, however, tremendous ; money fell short, and the great machine, the result of many years' labour and thought, has since been abandoned and broken up.

A far happier fate has so far attended the efforts of the brave young Brazilian, Albert Santos Dumont.   The wealthy son of a successful coffee-planter, he had always from his boyhood been keenly interested in aeronautics, and, coming to Paris, he constructed in 1898 an airship of a somewhat novel kind.   His balloon was cigar-shaped, 83 feet long, and holding 6500 feet of pure hydrogen.   Attached to the balloon, and working a propeller, was a small motor like those used for motor cycles, and astride of this Santos Dumont

SANTOS DUMONT'S AIRSHIP.

rode, bicycle fashion, steering his course with a rudder. In this ingenious machine he ascended from the Botanical Gardens in Paris and circled several times round the large captive balloon then moored there, after which he made a number of bold sweeps in the air, until an accident occurred to his engine and he came precipitately to the ground. Though shaken he was by no means discouraged, and declared his intention of continuing his experiments until he should have invented an airship which, in his own words, should be "not a mere plaything, but a practical invention, capable of being applied in a thoroughly useful fashion."

Accordingly he constructed one machine after another, gaining fresh knowledge by each new experience, and profiting by the accidents and failures which continually beset him in his dangerous and daring work. Before long also he received an additional incentive to his labours. Early in the year of 1900 it was announced by the Paris Aero Club, a society of Frenchmen interested in aeronautical matters, that one of its members, M. Deutsch, had offered a prize of 100,000 francs—about £4000—to the man who, starting from the Aero Club grounds at Longchamps in a balloon or flying machine, should steer his course right round the Eiffel Tower and back to the starting-place—a distance of three and a half miles—within half an hour. If the prize were not won within a certain time, his offer was to be withdrawn, and meanwhile he promised a certain sum of money every year for the encouragement of aeronautical experiments.

The offer of this reward set many inventors to work upon the construction of various aerial vessels of all kinds, but from the beginning Santos Dumont was well to the fore. By the middle of 1901 he had completed what was his sixth airship—a cigar-shaped balloon, 100 feet long, its propeller worked by a motor-car engine of fifteen horse-power—and with it, on July 15th, he made a splendid attempt for the prize. Starting from the Club grounds, he reached the Eiffel Tower in thirteen minutes, and, circling round it, started back on his homeward journey. But this time his voyage was against the wind, which was really too strong for the success of his experiment; part of his engine broke down, and the balance of the vessel became upset; and although he managed to fight his way back to the starting-point, he arrived eleven minutes behind time, and so failed to fulfil M. Deutsch's conditions.

Again, on the 9th of August, having in the meantime made further trials with his machine, he embarked on another attempt to carry off the prize. He chose the early hours of the morning, starting shortly after six from the Club grounds, where only a few friends, among them the keenly interested M. Deutsch, were present. The day was apparently perfect, and when, after the lapse of five minutes only, he had reached the Tower and swung gracefully round it, every one was convinced that this time the prize was certain to be won. But the homeward journey was all against the wind, which was blowing more powerfully aloft than on the ground, and suddenly the onlookers were horrified to see the fore part of the balloon double right back. By so doing the silken envelope became torn and the gas began escaping. Rapidly the balloon appeared to wither up and shrink together. The engine was seen still to be working, though no progress was now being made. Then the whole apparatus collapsed utterly, and fell with sickening speed upon the house-tops.

Deutsch and his companions watched the fall horror-struck, and jumping into their motorcars hurried to the spot, convinced that a fatal accident must have occurred. But they found that, although the airship was smashed to pieces, its plucky inventor had almost miraculously escaped unhurt. The wrecked machine had fallen upon the roof of a house in such a way that the keel had caught upon a corner, and the car, which was fastened to it, hung at a perilous angle down the side of a wall. Fortunately Dumont was secured to his car by a leather belt, and he managed to hold on, though in considerable danger lest the keel should break and let him fall, until rescued by a fireman with a rope. His machine was hopelessly ruined; but when asked what he intended to do next he merely answered : " Begin again. Only a little patience is necessary."

A new machine, "Santos Dumont VII.,"
was ready in less than a month, and tested on
the 6th of September. It behaved beautifully,
and all went well until the trail-rope caught
in a tree. In liberating it the framework became bent, and the airship was being towed
back to its shed when a sudden gust of wind
tore it away from those who held it. It immediately rose into the air, and on Dumont
opening the valve the whole collapsed and fell
to earth with a great shock. Again the lucky
inventor escaped unhurt, though owning this
time that he had "felt really frightened." Ten
days later, in another trial, the airship came
in contact with some trees, which pierced
the silk and let out the gas, so that it fell
precipitately twenty feet. But the aeronaut
appeared to bear a charmed life, for once more
he was none the worse for the fall. Several
other unsuccessful trials followed, and then,
on the 19th of October, Santos Dumont made
another grand attempt for the prize.

Starting with the wind in his favour, his
machine travelled at the rate of thirty miles
an hour, and rounded the Eiffel Tower in nine
minutes. But in the journey homewards the
airship had to struggle with a wind blowing
at thirteen miles an hour. In endeavouring
to "tack" the machinery became upset, and
Dumont, leaving his car, crawled along the
framework to the motor, which he succeeded
in putting in order again. But this naturally

occasioned some delay, and though he accomplished the rest of his journey in eight minutes, the Committee at first decided he had exceeded the allotted time by forty seconds, and so had lost the prize.   Great popular indignation was excited by this decision, for public sympathy was all with the daring and persistent young Brazilian, and M. Deutsch himself was most anxious he should receive the award.   Finally, he was considered to have fairly won it, and the money, which he afterwards divided among the poor, was formally presented to him.

Early in the next year Santos Dumont continued his experiments at Monaco, and on one occasion came down in the sea, and had to be rescued in the Prince of Monaco's own steam yacht.   After this there was a talk of further voyages being made in England, but the project came to nothing, and although Dumont made other ascents in Paris in the summer of 1903, he does not appear to have eclipsed his previous record.

But although Santos Dumont came through all his accidents and perils so happily, his example led to terrible disaster on the part of a luckless imitator.   In 1902 M. Severo, also a Brazilian, was fired with a desire to share his fellow-countryman's fame, and he also constructed an airship with which he proposed to do great things.   But while Dumont was a skilled aeronaut of large experience, as well as a mechanician, Severo

knew scarcely anything about the subject,
and had only been aloft once or twice. Proof
of his ignorance is shown by the fact that his
motor-engine was placed only a few feet away
from the valve through which the gas from
the balloon would escape.

The ascent took place in Paris early in the
morning of the 12th of May, and was witnessed, unhappily, by Severo's wife and son.
Bidding them good-bye, he stepped into the
car, and, accompanied by an assistant, rose
above the town. The balloon rose steadily,
and appeared to steer well. Then Severo
commenced to throw out ballast, and when
the airship had risen 2000 feet it was suddenly seen to burst into a sheet of flame
A terrible explosion followed, and then the
whole fell to the ground a hopeless wreck,
and the two men were dashed to pieces in the
fall. It is believed that this dreadful disaster,
which recalls the fate of Pilâtre de Rozier, was
caused by the hydrogen gas, which escaped
from the valve during the rapid rise, becoming
ignited by the engine, which, as has been said,
was placed dangerously close.

Nor was this, unhappily, the only accident
of the kind in Paris during the year. Only
five months later, on the 13th of October,
Baron Bradsky ascended with an assistant in
a large airship of his own invention. Through
faulty construction, the steel wires which fastened the car to the balloon broke, the two

became separated, the car fell, and its occupants were killed on the spot.

So far, the credit of the only English airship which has yet flown rests with Mr.
Stanley Spencer, the well-known aeronaut.
Mr. Spencer comes of a race of aeronauts.
His grandfather, Edward Spencer, was the
great friend and colleague of Charles Green,
and shared with him some of his chief ballooning adventures, notably the terrible voyage
when Cocking lost his life. Green stood
godfather to Edward Spencer's son, who was
christened Charles Green after him. He also
grew up to be an aeronaut, and made several
inventions and improvements relating to balloons and flying machines. His love of ballooning, inherited from his father, has been passed
on to his children, and his three eldest sons,
Percival, Arthur, and Stanley, are chief among
British aeronauts, and indeed have practically
the monopoly of professional ballooning and
balloon manufacture in Great Britain. Nor
have they confined themselves to this country.
All three have taken their balloons and parachutes to distant parts of the world, and
among their many hundreds of ascents, both
abroad and at home, have met with all manner
of exciting and perilous adventures, though
never yet with serious mishap. Their knowledge of practical aeronautics, then, is unrivalled, and Mr. Stanley Spencer had the
experience of three generations to guide

him when, in 1902, he set to work to build an airship which he had long been devising.

His first machine was a comparatively small one, capable only of lifting a light man. It took the usual form of a cigar-shaped balloon, the framework of which was built of bamboo, driven forward by a screw-propeller worked by a small petrol engine. Warned by the fate of the unfortunate Severo, Mr. Spencer placed his engine far away from the valve. Profiting also by Santos Dumont's experience, he constructed his balloon in such a manner that, should it become torn and the gas escape, the empty silk would collapse into the form of a parachute and break the fall. Furthermore, there was an arrangement by which, while aloft, ordinary air could be forced into the balloon to replace any loss of gas, and so keep the silk always fully inflated and "taut" —a very important factor in a machine that has to be driven forward through the atmosphere.

With this airship Mr. Spencer, as also his equally daring wife, made several highly successful trials at the Crystal Palace, when it was found to steer well and answer its helm most satisfactorily. Mr. Spencer also made two long voyages, from London and from Blackpool, on both of which occasions he found he could manœuvre his airship with considerable success, make circular flights,

and sail against the wind, provided it was
blowing only at moderate speed.

Encouraged by his success, he next built a
similar but much larger machine, nearly a
hundred feet long, holding 30,000 cubic feet
of gas, and driven by a petrol motor of twenty-
four horse-power. In this case the propeller, instead of being placed at the rear, as in general,
is at the front of the airship, thereby pulling
it forward through the air instead of pushing
it from behind. By this arrangement Mr.
Spencer thinks his balloon would have less
tendency to double up when urged against a
strong wind. The steering is done by a rudder
sail at the stern, and to cause his machine to
sail higher or lower, the aeronaut points its
head up or down by means of a heavy balance-
rope.

This new airship was ready by the summer
of 1903, but the unfavourable weather of that
stormy season again and again interfered with
the experiments. On the 17th of September
Mr. Spencer announced his intention of sailing
from the Crystal Palace round the dome of
St. Paul's, and returning to his starting-place.
The Cathedral was indeed safely reached, but
the increasing breeze, now blowing half a gale,
baffled all his attempts to circle round. Again
and again, till his hands were cut and bleeding
with the strain of the ropes, he brought his
machine up, quivering, to the wind, but all to
no purpose, until at length, abandoning the

attempt, he sailed with the current to Barnet. More favourable results may doubtless be looked for with better weather conditions.

In France during 1903 the brothers Lebaudy made some successful trips with an airship of their own construction. Many other airships are now being built in all parts of the world, in preparation for the aeronautical competitions to take place in America on the occasion of the St. Louis Exhibition of this year.

CHAPTER VII

THE FLYING MACHINE

It is now time we turn our attention from the airship to its important rival, the flying machine.

At first sight it may perhaps appear that so far the flying machine has accomplished less than the airship, and gives less promise of success, since up to the present time no flying machine has taken a man any distance into the air, or indeed done much more than just lift itself off the ground. Nevertheless those who have made a study of the matter are full of hope for the future. Many experts declare that already the limits of what can be done with the airship, which depends upon the lifting power of its gas to raise it and to sustain it in the air, are being reached. It has indeed been proved that on a calm day, or with only a light breeze, this form of sky vessel can be steered safely about the heavens, and doubtless as engines are constructed yet lighter and more powerful in proportion to their weight, more successful voyages still will be accomplished. But it is extremely doubtful whether an airship can ever be constructed which shall be able to stand against a gale of wind.

So long as a balloon sails only with the breeze it offers no resistance to the force of the wind, and can be made of the lightest and thinnest material. But directly it has to face the wind, and fight its way against it as an airship must do, then it has to be made of sufficient strength and rigidity to withstand the wind's power, or it will be blown to pieces. To make so large a thing as an airship withstand a rough wind, it must be built of very strong and rigid materials. To do this means to add to the weight of the machine. To lift the increased weight, a larger machine which can hold more gas is needed. The larger the machine the more surface it offers to the wind, and the stronger therefore must be its construction. It will now be seen that we are arguing in a circle, and we can understand that a point must be reached in the making of airships when, with our present materials, the advantage gained by increase of strength will be more than counterbalanced by increased weight. On this point Sir Hiram Maxim says: "It is not possible to make a balloon, strong enough to be driven through the air at any considerable speed, at the same time light enough to rise in the air; therefore balloons must always be at the mercy of a wind no greater than that which prevails at least 300 days in the year;" adding, "Those who seek to navigate the air by machines lighter than air have, I think, come practically to the end of their tether."

With the flying machine, on the contrary, the same difficulty does not arise. Since it is at all times heavier than air, and is kept aloft simply by its motive power and mechanism, its weight is of no consequence, provided only its engine is sufficiently powerful. It may, therefore, be built as rigidly as need be, while, from its size—which is much smaller in proportion to its lifting power than in the case of the airship—and also from its construction, it is much less liable to be affected by the wind.

In constructing a flying machine which is heavier than air the inventor has before him two examples of bodies which, though heavier than the atmosphere, yet contrive to rise upwards into the sky; these are, firstly, birds, and secondly, the familiar schoolboy toys, kites. To imitate the flying powers of birds and kites, he must first understand the means by which their flight is accomplished; and he will find, on examination, that to a large extent the same principle underlies each—the principle of what is termed the "aeroplane."

As we watch birds—especially large birds,

KESTREL.

as hawks and gulls—winging their way about the sky, we may notice that their flight is accomplished in two ways; either they are moving through the air by flapping their wings up and down, or else with wings wide outstretched they are soaring or sailing in the air for long times together without apparently moving their wings at all. Certain birds, such as vultures and albatrosses, possess this power of soaring flight to an extraordinary degree, and the exact way in which they keep themselves poised aloft is indeed still a mystery. We cannot, however, as we watch, say, a hawk, hovering in the air with motionless wing, help being struck by its resemblance to the schoolboy's kite, kept afloat high in the sky by the action of the wind properly applied to its surface, and we can at once see that the bird makes use of the same principle as the kite in its soaring or hovering flight. Indeed, just as a kite sinks to earth when the wind drops, so in a dead calm even an albatross has to flap its wings to keep afloat.

It is to the principle of the kite, therefore, that the inventor of the flying machine must turn. He must adapt the same principle to his apparatus, and this he does in his aeroplane, which, as will be seen, is an all-important part of his machine, and which, in its simplest form, is nothing more or less than a kite.

We know that if a light flat body, such as a kite, is lying upon the ground, and the wind gets under it so as to tilt it, it will be lifted by the wind into the air. The string of a kite is so adjusted that as the kite rises it is still held at an angle to the wind's force, and so long as the kite remains tilted at the necessary angle so long it will continue to rise or poise itself in the air while the wind blows. When schoolboys fly their kites they choose an exposed spot, and a day when the wind is blowing freshly and steadily. One boy throws the kite into the air, while another, holding the string to which it is fastened, draws it tight by running with it against the wind. By this means the kite, if rightly adjusted, is held at the proper angle to the wind, and started without dragging along the ground to begin with. As soon as the wind has fairly caught the kite and carried it up into the air, the boy who holds the string need run no longer, but if the breeze suddenly fails, and the kite begins to drop, he may still keep his toy aloft by running quickly along and dragging the kite after him; the artificial wind he thus creates making up for the lack of the other.

Now let us suppose that there is no string to hold the kite in proper position, and no boy to run with it; but that their places are supplied by a motor and propeller to drive it through the air; while at the same time it is so balanced as to preserve a fitting angle against a wind of its own making. We should then have a true flying machine, heavier than air, and yet capable of sailing through the sky.

This is the kind of flying machine that inventors at the present moment are trying to produce. They have, in their machines, to reproduce artificially two essential conditions that cause a kite to fly. They have to provide

a substitute for the strength of the wind, and
also a substitute for the pull of the string which
keeps the kite at the best angle to profit by
that strength.   The first they achieve by using
a suitable engine or motor, and the second by
supplying it with what are called " aeroplanes "
—large flat surfaces, light but rigid, inclined
at a suitable angle to the horizon.   By the use
of these the power of the engine is employed to
best advantage in causing the machine to sail
through the sky.

The great advantage of the aeroplane over
any other mode of flying is thus described by
Major Baden-Powell, one of our greatest living
authorities on aeronautical matters : " When
people realise that in the case of the aeroplane
a contrivance like the awning of a small steam
launch is capable of supporting the man and
the engines, and that in the case of the balloon
a mass like a big ship is necessary to lift the
same weight, one can readily understand the
advantages of the aeroplane, especially when
to the drawbacks of the bulky balloon are
added the great difficulties inherent in the
retention of a large volume of expensive,
inflammable, and subtle gas, ever varying in
its density."

The most successful inventors of flying
machines at the present day are all Americans,
though one of them has made his experiments
on this side of the Atlantic.   They are Sir
Hiram Maxim, inventor of the famous gun,

and one of the greatest mechanicians living;
Professor Langley, Secretary of the Smith-
sonian Institute, Washington; and the brothers
Wright.

Mr. Maxim, as he then was, commenced
his experiments in the early nineties. As
we have already shown, he went to Nature
for his guide, and in constructing his flying
machine took as his analogy the flight of
birds. Birds urge their way onwards in the
air by reason of the strength of their wings.
A flying machine must do the same by the
power of its engine; and as a bird's wings
must be strong in proportion to the bird's
weight, so the strength or horse-power of the
engine must stand in a certain proportion
to the number of pounds it weighs. Mr.
Maxim's first task, therefore, was to discover
what proportion this must be, and by his
experiments he arrived at a conclusion which
Professor Langley in America, working at
the same task at the same time, but quite
independently, had also proved to be true,
namely, that the faster a machine travels
through the air the greater·weight it may
carry; or, in other words, the quicker a body
moves through the atmosphere the less tendency will it have to fall to the ground. A
quick-flying bird like an albatross, therefore,
flies with less exertion, and so could carry a
greater weight, than a slow-moving bird like a
goose. It must therefore be to the advantage

of the flying machine that its engines should attain as great a speed as possible.

Maxim's next task was to construct a suitable engine. Light but powerful engines had not then reached the pitch of perfection they

THE MAXIM AIRSHIP.

have now, and his results proved at the time a perfect revelation of what could be done in this direction, and led to great advances being made.

Next came the designing of the great machine itself. It was an enormous apparatus, weighing over three tons, capable of carrying three men, and supported by no less than 4000

H

square feet of aeroplanes, placed one above the other. Its steam-engine was of 363 horse-power, and worked two screws of nearly 18 feet in diameter. Before such a machine could rise from the ground it must first have attained a very great forward impetus, and this it was to receive by running at a great speed on wheels along a railway track specially laid down for it. To prevent the apparatus rising unduly, a reversed rail was erected a short distance above, on which the machine would begin to run as soon as it lifted itself off the lower track. Along this railway the flying machine was tested, and it was found that as soon as a speed of thirty-six miles an hour was reached the wheels were lifted clear off the ground, and were running only upon the upper rail. On the last occasion a speed of forty-two miles an hour was attained, when the lifting power became so great that the restraining rail broke away altogether, and the great flying machine actually floated in the air for a few moments, "giving those on board the sensation of being in a boat," until, steam being shut off, it fell to the ground and was broken.

The enormous expense of his experiments has not prevented Sir Hiram Maxim from repeating them, and he hopes soon to have a much improved machine. Nevertheless his experience and calculations have been of great value to those who would follow in his footsteps, and have proved the possibility of constructing a flying machine which shall fly by virtue of its own motion.

Meanwhile in America Professor Langley was experimenting, independently, almost on the same lines. He also was bent on producing a flying machine, but instead of starting to work upon a large apparatus like Maxim, he began by making models, and gradually worked his way up to bigger things. For many months he studied to understand the principle of those ingenious little toys sometimes seen, which, by means of the tension of a twisted india-rubber band, will keep afloat in the air for a few seconds. Next he constructed small models driven by steam, in which he found his great difficulty was in keeping down the weight. For years he persevered in his work without any great success, until in 1896 he produced a model machine which he called an "aerodrome." It was quite small, weighing with its engine only 25 lbs., and measuring but 14 feet from tip to tip of its aeroplanes. The experiments were made over water, and the necessary momentum was given by dropping it from a platform 20 feet high. On more than one occasion this little flying machine rose with great steadiness in the face of the wind to a height of 100 feet, moving so smoothly that it might have carried a glass of water without spilling a drop; and then, the steam of its engine being exhausted, sank down gracefully upon the water, having flown about half a mile in a minute and a half. This success encouraged Professor Langley next to construct a full-sized flying machine on the same lines; but this on its first voyage plunged headlong into the water and was hopelessly damaged. The United States Government have since granted him a sum of money to continue his experiments.

Latest of all the airship inventors, and perhaps so far the most successful, are the brothers Wright. Up to the date of writing this the full details of their work are not yet made public, but it is known that on the 17th of December 1903, their machine, which consists of two large aeroplanes driven forward by an engine of sixteen horse-power, after being started along a short track on level ground, rose into the air and flew for about half a mile.

It remains for us now to make brief mention of how men have tried, and are still trying, to imitate the soaring or gliding flight of birds without the use of machinery to assist them. We have seen how an albatross can, when the wind is blowing, convert itself, as it were, into a kite, and keep aloft in the air for a while without moving its wings. Similarly many people have attempted, by attaching themselves to a large supporting surface or aeroplane, and casting themselves off from a height, to glide with the wind across wide stretches of country. In this mode of soaring flight some have made considerable progress. Herr Lilienthal, a German, was perhaps for a time the most successful. He started from small beginnings, jumping off a spring board a few feet high, and gradually increasing the height as he became more accustomed to his apparatus. Later he had a large artificial mound made specially for him, and from the top of this he would throw himself into the air, and with a favourable wind sail a distance of four hundred yards at a considerable height above the ground. Lilienthal's experiments, however, came to a sad end. On August the 11th, 1896, after he had glided along in the air for about two hundred yards, a sudden gust of wind caught the wide-spread wings of his apparatus, and tilted it upwards. This caused him to lose his balance, and he fell from a height of sixty feet and broke his spine. A similar accident also caused the death, a few years later, of a young Englishman, Mr. Percy S. Pilcher, who had been following up Lilienthal's experiments.

The greatest difficulty now to be overcome in solving the problem of human flight, whether with soaring apparatus or flying machine, may be summed up in one word—"balance." Every schoolboy knows that the great art of kite-flying consists in so adjusting the point of attachment of the string and the length of the tail that his kite is properly balanced, and is not liable to turn over or "dip" when in the air. Every observer of birds, too, has noticed how largely the question of balance enters into their flying. A bird in the air is continually and instinctively adjusting its wings to its position, and to every puff of wind, even as a man on a bicycle is continually, though unconsciously, adjusting his handle-bar to the inequalities of the road; and as a cyclist requires practice before he can ride his machine, or a skater before he can keep his feet on the ice, so even a bird has to learn how to balance itself before it can use its wings.

Dwellers in the country are familiar with the way in which the parent birds teach their fledglings to fly, instructing them by example, and encouraging them in their first short flights until they have become familiar with their powers and can balance themselves aright in the air. And if even birds, with whom flying is an instinct, have to learn the art of balancing themselves in the air by practice, how much. more so must such a clumsy creature as a man, to whom flying is entirely unnatural. Only by long and painful efforts can he ever hope to succeed at all, and unfortunately all such efforts are necessarily very dangerous. Many disastrous accidents have already occurred, and although great progress has been made, and the time may not now be far distant when, by means of improved machines, men will actually fly, it will

be at the cost of much labour, and, it is to
be feared, at the sacrifice of many more
brave lives.

CHAPTER VIII

CONCLUSION

IN our last chapters we have, in some measure,
brought our aeronautical history up to the
present day, though of necessity many important points and notable voyages have been
passed over unnoticed. It now remains to us
but to gather up the loose ends of the story,
and then briefly to indicate the direction in
which we may expect new advances in the
future.

And, first of all, it may be well to mention
a few ballooning "records." The largest
balloon ever known was used as a captive
at the Paris Exhibition of 1878. It was of
883,000 cubic feet capacity, and capable of
lifting more than fifty passengers at a time.
Other mammoth balloons of almost as great
dimensions have also been employed for captive
work; but the largest balloon intended specially
for "right away" ascents was the "Giant,"
built in Paris in 1863 by M. Nadar. It held
215,000 cubic feet of gas, and was made of
22,000 yards of best white silk, at 5s. 4d. a

yard. The car was particularly elaborate, almost as big as a small cottage, being of two stories, and divided into several rooms. It proved, however, to be a very dangerous adjunct, for on the two occasions it was used those within received very serious injury during rough landings, and it was soon put aside and replaced by an ordinary basket. None of these monster sky craft appear to have been very successful, and at the present day the largest balloons in general use do not exceed 50,000 or 60,000 cubic feet capacity.

The honour of the longest aerial voyage ever made rests with the unfortunate Andrée, who, if his dates are to be relied upon, had been forty-eight hours aloft in his balloon when he despatched his last found message. Not far behind in point of time, however. was Count de la Vaulx, who in the summer of 1901 attempted to cross the Mediterranean by balloon. Contrary winds in the end baffled his venture, and he was forced to descend on the deck of a steamer which was following his course, but not before he had spent forty-one hours in the sky. The year previous the Count had also achieved a record long-distance voyage in connection with some balloon competitions held during the French "Exposition" of 1900. Starting from Paris, he descended in Russia, 1193 miles away, having been aloft thirty-six hours all but fifteen minutes.

For lofty ascents the palm still rests with

Glaisher and Coxwell, whose famous voyage of 1862, when, as related, a height of 37,000 feet (or seven miles) is said to have been reached, has never been equalled. The exact altitude attained on this occasion is, however, as we have explained, only conjectural, neither being capable at the last of taking observations, and no height being *registered* over 29,000 feet. On July 31st, 1901, two German scientists, Dr. Berson and Dr. Suring, ascended from Berlin to a *registered* altitude of 34,400 feet, or well over six miles. They were provided with compressed oxygen to breathe, but even then became unconscious during the last 800 feet of the ascent. Three years before Dr. Berson had made a very lofty ascent in England, accompanied by Mr. Stanley Spencer, when a height of 27,500 feet was reached. A terrible accident occurred in connection with a lofty scientific ascent made from Paris in 1875 by Tissandier, inventor of the airship already mentioned, and two companions. Their object was to attain a record height, in which they indeed succeeded, reaching 28,000 feet. But despite the artificial air they took with them to breathe, they all three became unconscious in the extreme upper regions, and when, after one of the most awful voyages in the whole history of ballooning, Tissandier came to himself, it was to find the bodies of his two friends stiff and cold beside him in the car.

Coming to the aeronautical work of the present day, it is humiliating to have to confess that, through lack of public support, England has somewhat fallen behind other nations. In America and on the Continent large sums of money are subscribed for experiments with balloons, airships, and flying machines; but in our own country all efforts in these directions are due to private enterprise alone. Among those most keenly interested in aeronautical progress may be mentioned Mr. P. Alexander, of Bath; Major Baden-Powell, President of the English Aeronautical Society; and the Rev. J. M. Bacon. The latter has made many scientific balloon ascents for the study of meteorology, acoustics, and other kindred sciences, and his observations have proved of much interest and value. During his voyages he has met with several adventures, though no serious mishaps. On one occasion, when the writer accompanied him, during a night ascent made to observe the great shower of Leonid shooting stars foretold for the 16th of November 1899, the balloon became unmanageable while lost above the clouds. For ten hours it refused to come down, during much of which time the sea was heard beneath, and the voyagers believed themselves blown out over the Atlantic. A very stormy landing, in which the writer broke her arm, was eventually made near the coast in South Wales as before mentioned.

In November 1902, Mr. Bacon, accompanied by Mr. Percival Spencer, crossed the Irish Channel by balloon, the second time only this dangerous passage has been made, the first occasion being the voyage of Mr. Windham Sadler, eighty-five years before. Mr. Bacon's voyage was partly undertaken for the Admiralty, who lent the services of a gunboat to follow the balloon's course over the sea. One of the special objects of investigation was to test a theory, long held, that from a considerable height aloft the bottom of the sea becomes visible, even in rough weather when the surface is troubled with waves. This point was very successfully settled, for although the sea was very rough, Mr. Bacon not only saw, but succeeded in photographing, from a height of 600 feet, the beds of sand and rock lying in ten fathoms at the bottom of the Irish Channel—a feat never before accomplished.

In scientific observations of the upper atmosphere a valuable ally to the balloon has been found in the kite. The making of kites has now reached a high pitch of perfection, and by their means self-recording scientific instruments can be raised to vast heights in the air, and even men carried aloft with safety. A kite which latterly has excited much attention is the Cody kite. With this, during the autumn of 1903, its inventor, a Mexican, hazarded a bold venture. Harnessing it to a light boat, and waiting for a favourable wind, he started from Calais at eight o'clock one November evening, and was safely towed all night across the Channel, reaching Dover at five the next morning.

The aeronautical competitions at the St. Louis Exhibition, in America, have given a great impetus to one branch at least of aeronautics, while the labour of many scientific workers throughout the whole world is directed to the improvement of our present modes of exploring the heavens, and the turning to best account of the means already at our disposal. Never since the days when the Montgolfier brothers floated their first frail craft has so much interest as now been manifested in the conquest of the sky, and never has progress been more rapid and sure. Whether the day will ever come when man will rule the atmosphere as he now does the sea is, as yet, uncertain, but there are many who hope and believe not only that he will, but that the day is not far distant when the birds will no longer hold undisputed sway over the empire of the air.